HOW TO WRITE THE PERFECT RESUME

400 PX

1365 PX

DISCLAIMER

The information contained in this book is based on personal experience and anecdotal evidence and is for educational purposes only. Although the author has made every reasonable attempt to achieve complete accuracy of the content in this product, he assumes no responsibility for errors or omissions.

You should use this information as you see fit and at your own risk. Everyone's situation is unique, and applying the information found in this book in no way guarantees employment or any other result desired from reading this book. The author assumes no responsibility or liability whatsoever on the behalf of the purchaser or reader of these materials.

ABOUT THE AUTHOR

Dan Clay is a writer, author and sales professional based in San Francisco, CA. Over the past ten years, his resume has landed him jobs across a broad spectrum of companies, from a five-person startup incubated by the prestigious Y-Combinator to global powerhouses such as Shell, LinkedIn, Google, and Gartner—the latter two listed on Glassdoor's Top 25 Companies That Give the Toughest Job Interviews.

Through a series of strategic career moves, Dan grew his income over sixfold in just four years, and soon after founded The Conscious Career, a place where he writes about how to approach your career in a more mindful, deliberate way. He is the author of *How to Write The Perfect Resume* and has become a sought-after resource for everything from resume writing to interviewing and salary negotiation.

You can follow Dan on LinkedIn at www.linkedin.com/in/danclay and subscribe to The Conscious Career newsletter by visiting www.danclay.com/signup.

TABLE OF CONTENTS

FREE BONUS MATERIALS

As my way of saying thanks for picking up this book, I'm making several bonus materials available absolutely free just for readers of *How to Write the Perfect Resume* that will dramatically enhance your ability to execute the strategies outlined in this book.

Here's what I'm offering:

- Five customizable, fully editable resume templates in Microsoft Word format that have been tested and proven to land interviews at world-class organizations

- 77 Hard-Hitting Resume Action Verbs and Phrase Examples in PDF format to help you build powerful resume bullets that will instantly grab attention

- The 66-Point Perfect Resume Checklist in PDF format to make sure your resume is absolutely perfect before sending to recruiters and hiring managers

- A Before & After Resume Transformation example to see the difference between a resume that recruiters pass over versus one they can't ignore

- To access these FREE bonus materials, simply visit www.danclay.com/perfectresume, enter your name and email address, and click the button to submit.

SIGN UP FOR THE CONSCIOUS CAREER NEWSLETTER

Feeling unfulfilled in your career? If so, sign up for the Conscious Career newsletter by heading over to www.danclay.com/signup.

Whether you're planning a career change, looking for ways to improve in the job you already have, or simply trying to figure out what you want to do with your life, my weekly newsletter covers all that and more. Every week, you'll receive my latest insights, strategies, and resources designed to help you take control of your career and discover more joy and meaning from your life's work.

Visit www.danclay.com/signup to start receiving the Conscious Career newsletter today!

CHAPTER 1

RESUME REALITIES AND WHY I WROTE THIS BOOK

There's no shortage of information out there covering how to write a better resume—just Google "resume writing tips" and you'll see nearly 3 million *pages* of search results! With so many sources of advice and recommendations, you'd think everyone's resumes would be perfect by now, right?

Think again.

How do I know? Aside from the fact that I've personally reviewed my fair share of terrible resumes, the fact remains that there are far more people who *fail* to land a job than there are those who succeed. One study found that for every job opening a company posts, it receives 250 resumes[1]. Of these, only one will be offered the job. That's a 99.6% failure rate among those who submit their resumes—more than adequate to define the status quo.

Most people only think about their resumes when it's time to look for another job, and with the average worker staying at a job for 4.4 years, almost half a decade can go by before they give their resume so much as a second thought. Nor should they! Your resume is like a fire extinguisher—you only really think about it when you need it. And while your resume may not mean the difference between life and death, it can certainly mean the difference between feast or famine—or landing your dream job versus a job that you dread getting up for every morning.

When it finally comes time to dust off the old resume, most people do the same thing: Google a few relevant search terms, collect some advice from the top page search results, add their most recent work experience, and start firing off those job applications. By taking the same approach, most people end up among the 99.6% of applicants who fail to land the jobs they apply for.

With such intense competition vying for each job opening, having a resume that stands out from the pack is critical. You'll rarely get a second chance to make a first impression, and mistakes can mean the difference between getting called for an interview or your resume being thrown in the trash pile and your dream job going up in smoke.

It's hard to make your resume shine brighter than the rest when you're using the same bland, generic advice that everybody else is. And with something as important as the future of your career, why should you settle for having your resume be anything less than the best it can possibly be? When you have to summarize the entirety of your life's achievements onto a single piece of paper, shouldn't it tell a powerful story about you that makes people yearn to know more?

Crafting a resume that will get you noticed is easier than you think as long as you follow the right steps. The problem with using information from across the Internet is that it will get you 85% of the way to a great resume—but a truly great resume requires that you get 100% of the way there. That, and it's hard to tell who you can trust. Should you really bank the future of your career on a junior staff writer who's padding articles with keywords to drive up the Google rankings of the blog he's writing them for?

I decided to write this book to address a consistent need I saw among family, friends and acquaintances for solid, practical resume advice from someone who's actually used it to land lucrative job offers from world-class companies. There's no shortage of recruiters turned "talent coaches" offering their guidance based on what they've seen on the receiving end, but the mindset of someone quickly scanning through dozens or hundreds of resumes on a daily basis is miles away from that of a job seeker, who puts his hopes and dreams on the line with every resume he sends. Plus, asking a recruiter how to land your dream job is kind of like asking a talent scout how to hit a homerun. They can talk through the mechanics all day long, but when it comes time to step up to the plate and show you how it's done, they can't back up the talk with an equally compelling walk.

So who am I, and what makes *me* qualified to write about writing resumes? First, a few words on who I'm *not*. I'm not a self-proclaimed "guru" who's recently decided to do some research about a topic and write a book about it. Nor am I some lifelong career coach who's never held a job in a recognizable company yet purports to understand how to get hired into one. I'm not an ex-recruiter trying my hand at the professional training racket. So, who am I?

In all likelihood, I'm probably a lot like you. I work at a decent-sized company, get paid a steady salary and answer to a manager. I have quarterly goals to hit, complain when HR sends out mandatory training modules, and receive a ridiculous amount of email. If that all sounds familiar, that's because it is—I just happen to know how to put together a phenomenally well-executed resume, and I've used it to land job offers from some of the most well-known and highly respected companies in the world.

Over the past decade, my resume has landed me jobs across a broad spectrum of companies, from a five-person startup incubated by the prestigious Y-Combinator to global powerhouses such as Shell, Google, LinkedIn, and Gartner. Two of these, Gartner and Google, were ranked number four and number eight respectively in Glassdoor's <u>Top 25 Companies That Give the Toughest Job Interviews</u>[2]. When it comes to cracking tough organizations, my resume has gone through the paces and come out the other side with the battle scars to prove it.

I know what you're thinking—with all those high profile names on my resume, how could it *not* attract the attention of recruiters? Well, it wasn't always that way, and before I landed a job offer at Google, I had absolutely zero experience working for technology companies. Zilch. Nada. It must have been that pricey Ivy League degree that drew them in then, right? Nope—I went to a public university (Go Spartans!). And, before you pin the reason on my fortunate connections, I have to point out that none of my friends or relatives worked at Google at the time I applied. Believe me, as much as I would have loved to have skated into an interview there, that wasn't the case—my resume and experience had to stand on their own.

The good news for you is that if I could do it, you can too. You don't need the blessing of lucky life circumstances to get to where you want to go—just a set of proven practices and a masterful approach to positioning yourself. This book is designed to be a complete resource for making your resume the best it can be, worthy of consideration at the most prestigious of companies. I can't guarantee that it will get you hired, as I've had my share of rejections too—but I *can* promise that it will elevate your resume to an elite level of professionalism that few can claim.

In the following sections, we'll cover things like:

- How to strike a proper balance between content and whitespace
- The four tests your resume must pass in order to land you an interview
- 77 examples of powerful action statements to showcase your professional experience
- How to make your accomplishments sound more impressive without lying about them
- The Ten Golden Rules of resume writing
- How to explain gaps in your work history
- A Before & After resume example
- Common resume mistakes to avoid
- The finishing touches that most people don't pay attention to

- Five battle-tested resume templates you can use right now

I wrote this book to be as information dense as possible with a single goal in mind: to land you interviews at companies you're interested in working for. I understand how frustrating it can be to get your hopes up for a particular job only to never hear a peep from the company you've applied to. After this happens a few times, your hopes start to fade and you go numb to the implicit rejection that happens day after day.

If that's where you are now, I have one thing to say to you: you're much better than you give yourself credit for. Simply taking the initiative to purchase this book means that you're seizing ownership and accountability for the outcome you desire and are prepared to take the steps necessary to get there. That puts you ahead of most people who drift aimlessly through the job search process hoping that one day, lightning will strike. It doesn't work that way—in order to get the job you want, you have to *earn* it first. And that starts with taking responsibility for creating the life you want for yourself.

Are you ready to take your resume to the next level and get one step closer to landing the job you've always dreamed of? It's time to roll up your sleeves and break out your A-game. Let's go!

-Dan

CHAPTER 2

FOUR BASIC RESUME TRUTHS

Let's start by touching on a few basic truths about resumes.

RESUME TRUTH #1

If you hope to land the job you want, you absolutely need a resume.

Despite the dramatic advancements in technology that have transformed society over the last several decades, the good old fashioned resume remains the standard by which companies filter, select, and hire candidates for job openings. Regardless of how creatively you may want to express your accomplishments to your desired employer, the fact is that if you don't have a standard resume, you have little to no chance of being seriously considered for a position. Your LinkedIn profile, blog, portfolio or other information can be useful, but without a resume you're dead in the water.

There are good reasons for this, too—one being that the company needs to CYA (if you're unfamiliar with the acronym, check out the top Google search result) in case any lawsuits pop up as a result of the candidate handling process. Companies need a universally recognized, formal document that they can reference to protect themselves against any claims of ageism, sexism, racism, or other charges tying failure to hire a candidate to anything other than the candidate not being qualified for the role. That, and all the expensive HR and recruiting software they've invested in is built to handle standard resumes.

Long story short? You need a resume. But since you've purchased this book, you already knew that, right?

And while you may consider it a shame to be held to a convention that began over half a century ago, the status quo holds a certain truth that makes it extremely beneficial to the candidate who can properly exploit it.

Which truth is that?

RESUME TRUTH #2

Most people's resumes suck.

The truth is, most people's resumes fail to meet even the minimum bar for professionalism. They're sloppy, disorganized, rambling, illogical, confusing, and any number of other negative adjectives useful for describing their state of inadequacy. That's good news for you, because by simply having a resume that passes a few basic requirements, you'll already be head and shoulders above most of the others out there. This book is designed to go above and beyond that minimum bar, however, and bring your resume into the top 1% of every resume in circulation.

At this point, you may be thinking that there's no way your resume could ever be considered among the top 1% of those out there—surely there are thousands, if not millions, of candidates who have accomplished more, have a more advanced degree from a better school, have worked for more prestigious companies, and are just generally more appealing to potential employers than you are, right?

Before you start to go down this path of self-doubt, allow me to introduce Truth #3:

RESUME TRUTH #3

How you communicate and position your accomplishments is more important than what you've actually accomplished.

Perception is reality, and you alone have the power—and some might argue, the responsibility—to shape the perception that you wish to convey. It doesn't matter if someone else discovered the cure for cancer and single-handedly doubled her company's stock price in the span of a week—if her resume exhibits poor communication, is riddled with typos, and generally looks sloppy, then that person will get passed over for someone with more modest achievements but whose resume is sharp, polished, and professional. Guaranteed.

Now, that doesn't mean that you should lie on your resume—quite the contrary. Lying on your resume invites all kinds of traps and complications that could spring on you at any moment and destroy both your shot at landing the job and your professional credibility. However, you have complete control over how you choose to position yourself in the eyes of the person reading your resume. And when you position yourself to stand out, recruiters won't have any choice but to take notice.

Which brings me to Truth #4:

RESUME TRUTH #4

Recruiters want the same thing you do: To find the best person for the job (ideally, you!) as quickly and as cheaply as possible.

Recruiters, like salespeople, have quotas for how many job openings they need to fill in a certain period of time. I've never been a recruiter, but I have been in sales for almost a decade, so I have a thorough understanding of what it means to have to hit a quota. Of the large quantity of resumes a recruiter will process, a handful will turn into phone screens, a smaller number will move to the interview stage, an even smaller number will result in job offers, and depending on whether or not any offers are rejected, a potentially smaller number still will actually end up as hires. That's a lot of work that the recruiter has to go through for what could be only a handful of filled job openings (and, in some cases—none at all).

This winnowing of candidates at each stage in the hiring process is referred to as the candidate pipeline, which is illustrated below:

The Candidate Pipeline

On average, a company will receive around 250 resumes for every job opening they have available. A whopping 75% of these resumes will be from candidates who aren't actually qualified to do the job![3] When you combine the fact that recruiters receive a huge number of resumes on a daily basis with the truth that most resumes aren't fit for consideration, you come away with a tremendous rejection bias on the part of the recruiter.

When a recruiter picks up your resume, they're immediately scanning it for the obvious mistakes that everybody else makes and expecting to move it into the rejection pile before moving on to more promising opportunities. Recruiters are lazy this way out of necessity—if they took the time to carefully scrutinize every resume that came across their desk, they'd be out of a job.

Because they're so used to seeing half-hearted rubbish, coming across a good resume to them is like finding a $50 bill on the ground—it fills them with excitement for the prospect of being one step closer to meeting the ever-looming quota hanging over their head.

Keeping these four truths in mind as you build out your resume will help you mold it into the needle in a haystack that will put a smile on the faces of every recruiter who picks it up. And giving the recruiter a reason to smile is definitely a position you want to find yourself in!

CHAPTER 3

YOUR TARGET AUDIENCE AND THE FOUR TESTS YOUR RESUME MUST PASS

Your resume has one purpose: to land you a job interview.

Obviously, getting hired for the job you want is your ultimate goal, but your resume is the crucial first step on the way there. And its job is to get your foot in the door and open up a dialogue with the recruiter looking to fill the position. To do that, you need to demonstrate that you possess the required skills for the job you're applying for. Remember, the recruiter's goal is to find the best person for the job as quickly and as cheaply as possible, which brings me to the first Golden Rule of resume writing:

RESUME GOLDEN RULE #1

Only write your resume for job openings you're qualified to fill.

It may sound obvious, but as the previously mentioned statistic shows, a shockingly high number of people still apply for jobs they haven't the slightest qualifications for. Maybe they think that the more resumes they submit, the greater the chances someone will call them back. This is highly unprofessional and a waste of everyone's time. Make sure you have a clear understanding of the position you're applying for and feel confident that you'd be successful should you be hired.

There are four key audiences that you need to consider when writing your resume:

1. **Applicant Tracking Software (ATS):** Companies (especially large ones) use software to filter resumes by how closely their content matches the keywords contained in the job descriptions the resumes are being submitted for. That means you'll need to tailor your resume content to ensure that it doesn't get filtered into the "no" pile.

2. **Recruiters:** These are the actual humans who will read your resume after the ATS has worked its magic. They may see hundreds of resumes in a single day, so yours has to strike a positive first impression right away.

3. **Interviewers:** Should you be invited to an interview or phone screen, your interviewer may have a copy of your resume in front of them during the interview to help guide their questions. You should be prepared to explain every point on your resume in greater detail if you're asked to.

4. **The Hiring Manager:** The hiring manager often holds more power over the hiring decision than anyone else in the organization, so your resume really needs to reflect the skills and capabilities that the hiring manager is looking for.

In addition to these key audiences, there are four tests your resume must pass in sequential order before it can achieve your goal of landing a job interview:

1. **The Keyword Test:** The first line of defense your resume must break through is the company's ATS system. Including keywords in your resume that match the keywords in the job description will ensure that your resume will come out the other side ready for a human to put his eyes on it.

2. **The Scan Test:** Because recruiters are used to seeing such terrible resumes, they're going to automatically assume that yours falls into this category as well. In order to quickly filter out this inadequate majority, they'll be scanning for obvious reasons for disqualification within a matter of seconds. When a recruiter picks it up, your resume's first job is to sell the recruiter on reading it in closer detail. If your resume performs this job well, then you're already ahead of most people whose resumes don't.

3. **The Qualifications Test:** After your resume passes the scan test, the recruiter will be looking to see if you meet the basic qualifications outlined for the role such as education, years of experience, skills, etc. This is why it's so important to only apply for jobs you're qualified for—failing the qualifications test is immediate grounds for getting your resume placed into the rejection pile.

4. **The Fit Test:** By the time your resume passes the qualifications test, the recruiter will be pretty excited about finding a potential candidate for the role. At this stage, they *really* want to put you into their candidate pipeline, but they still need to make sure that you'd be a good potential fit. This is where they'll look more closely at how you communicate your professional experience and the overall level of professionalism that you convey. Once you pass this test, you're golden—your name goes into their system as a viable opportunity and they put you in line for a phone screen.

Understanding the different tests your resume must pass is important because each phase of resume development will be used to pass one or more of these tests. Knowing which of the tests each phase will help you pass provides key context to help you craft a more well-rounded resume. Most people's resumes don't pass all of these tests, which is why most get passed over. By applying the lessons in this book, your resume is going to pass these tests with flying colors!

Should you write a cover letter?

Cover letters are largely an antiquated relic of a time gone by. There are far more effective ways of penetrating an organization than blindly submitting your resume and cover letter through the organization's careers page. Only 17% of recruiters even bother reading them anyway[4], so you're better off not wasting your time. When you think about it, it makes sense—recruiters already have dozens of resumes to go through every day, so why would they want to add another layer of processing on top of that? Plus, having to write a custom cover letter for every job you apply to could take hours of extra time. Do yourself a favor and skip the cover letter.

The one exception to this rule is if you're unable to find another way into the company through a mutual connection, cold outreach or referral and are forced to submit your resume and cover letter through the company's career page as a last resort. This is the Hail Mary of the job search world and should be avoided at all costs. Your chances of success are much lower when you use this method, but they're better than not submitting anything at all. However, because you can *almost always* find a way to bypass the traditional means of applying for a job, you'll rarely if ever need a cover letter, which is why I chose to leave them out of this book.

CHAPTER 4

PLANNING AND OUTLINING YOUR RESUME

The Fundamentals

Your resume is one of the few things in your life that needs to be absolutely perfect. According to a CareerBuilder survey, 61% of recruiters will disqualify a resume that contains even a *single* typo[5]. And because you'll potentially be competing with hundreds of other resumes, yours needs every edge it can get. Don't let this scare you, though—if you follow the best practices in this book, your resume will be more than prepared to stand against the toughest adversaries.

When writing your resume, think of yourself as a product and your resume as a marketing document selling the virtues of that product. The company you're applying to is the potential buyer, and you need to convince that company that you're the best possible product they could buy out of all the options available. You don't necessarily need to close them yet—that's what the interview is for—but you should make them sufficiently interested in learning more about how "you the product" can deliver value to their company. Put yourself in the recruiter's shoes—if you picked up your resume, would *you* want to hire you?

Your resume is the physical representation of your most important professional achievements, so it should invoke a sense of confidence and expertise in whoever's reading it. It should be crisp, concise, and visually appealing. You should unapologetically stand behind and be prepared to defend everything you choose to include in it. It shouldn't be an extensive list of everything you've ever done, either—remember, recruiters are overwhelmed with the amount of resumes they have to deal with, so yours needs to pack a strong punch in an extremely small amount of time. Your choice of words should be straightforward and impactful without being unnecessarily pretentious or overly flowery.

Planning Your Resume

I can't blame you if you're struggling to decide which pieces of information to include in your resume—staring at a blank page of infinite possibilities is enough to leave anyone feeling at least a little overwhelmed. But fret not, because the dirty little secret of writing great resume content lies right under your nose!

Before you dive into writing your resume, you need to carefully consider who you're writing it for. Remember, you're trying to sell a product—you—so you need to know what your potential buyer—the company—cares about most. And where do you find such information? Why, the job description, of course! Enter Resume Golden Rule #2:

RESUME GOLDEN RULE #2

Build your resume to reflect the language used in your target job descriptions.

As the first Golden Rule states, you should only submit your resume for positions that you're qualified to fill. Doing so will allow you to focus on opportunities for which you're best suited and help you hone your resume to be the perfect fit for what the recruiter is looking for.

Your resume must first pass the keyword test administered by a company's ATS filter before it can move to the next stage of consideration. Failing this test most likely means getting sucked into the feared resume "black hole", where you never hear a peep from the company after you submit it (we've all been there, and yes, it sucks). By closely reflecting the verbiage of the job descriptions you're targeting, your resume can avoid being pulled past the event horizon and live to see the light of another day.

The first order of business in the resume planning process is to prepare your work environment. You'll need the following items:

- A computer (laptop or desktop)
- A blank word document (Word, Google Doc, Evernote, etc.—pick your poison)
- Your preferred web browser
- Internet access

Crafting an amazing resume requires a fair amount of concentration, so make sure your surroundings are conducive to wiring in and getting focused. Whether this happens to be in a coffee shop, home office, or on a plane, all that matters is that you feel energized to do great work.

Once you're situated, open up your blank word document and name it something like "Resume Planning Document". Or, if you prefer something a bit less vanilla, you can give it a name like "Global Domination Document to Strike Fear into the Hearts of My Enemies." Either way works!

Create the following four headings within the blank document and space them out on the page:

- Companies
- Roles
- Job Posting URLs
- Keywords & Themes

Next, resize the word document window so it takes up half of the screen (if you have dual monitors, pick a monitor to assign the word document to). Then, open up your web browser and resize it to fill the other half of the screen (with dual monitors, put the browser on the monitor opposite the word document).

The end result should look something like this:

Now you're cooking with fire!

Step one in the keyword planning process is to take an inventory of the positions you're interested in. Start by listing both the companies you're interested in working for and the titles of the specific roles you're interested in applying for under the "Companies" and "Roles" headings. You may have already done some of this legwork, and that's fine—no need to duplicate efforts. If you haven't started researching jobs yet, that's fine too—simply make a note of any interesting companies and roles as you go.

Next, visit the careers pages of those companies and see what kind of openings they have available. Note any roles you're interested in along with the URL of each job posting under the "Job Posting URLs" heading of your planning doc so you can refer back to them when you need to. Once you've built your list of target jobs, you're ready to move onto the final phase of the planning process.

This phase involves wrapping your head around the various skills and capabilities that you'll need to communicate on your resume in order to pass the keyword/ATS test as well as the other recruiter tests. Go through each of the job description pages and make a note of the common keywords you see across them under the "Keywords and Themes" heading of your planning doc.

This is where the side-by-side windows come in—arranging the windows this way makes it incredibly easy to copy phrases from a job description right into the planning doc without having to minimize and reopen them. I encourage you to use the copy and paste functions liberally in this phase!

The words and themes you pull from your target job descriptions will form the foundation of the achievements you'll highlight throughout your resume to demonstrate your suitability for the role. Here's a simplified version of what your planning document might look like when you're finished:

RESUME PLANNING DOCUMENT

Companies I'm interested in:

- Google
- Oracle
- Netsuite
- SAP

Potential roles:

- Account Manager
- Customer Success Manager
- Client Representative

URLs for job openings:

indeed.com/jobnumberoneexample

oracle.com/jobs/na/sales/12749301.html

google.com/careers/461239

google.com/careers/384640

Keywords/Phrases:

"Managing client relationships"

"Ensure customer satisfaction"

Proven ability to lead clients through the process of articulating business goals, establishing success metrics, and achieving results

Passionate about delighting clients and driving real business results

The keyword planning phase is absolutely *crucial* in the resume writing process because it puts you in the mindset of tailoring your resume for a specific purpose rather than randomly listing your accomplishments and hoping you catch the recruiter's attention. These companies are literally telling you what they're looking for, so give them what they want! You'll be surprised at how much more confident you feel once you've completed this step because you'll have essentially taken the mystery out of the equation around what to put into your resume. You know what they want, so now all you have to do is figure out how to give it to them (which, admittedly, is easier said than done).

So you've outlined your planning document and have a solid grasp of what you need to include in your resume. Time to start building it out, right? Not so fast. Before you start working on your formal resume document, you first need to put some intense thought into which professional achievements you can draw from that match the key themes from your target job descriptions and position you best for the role.

This is the *single* most difficult and time-consuming part of the resume writing process, and it's also the most important.

At this stage, you're still in brainstorming mode, so it helps not to have a formal structure restricting your thought process. You can use the following questions to help you uncover the accomplishments that may or may not end up in your resume. Try not to apply any judgement or filtering during this process; list everything out as it comes to you and the filtering will come later.

Questions to guide resume content:

- If you had 30 seconds in an elevator with the CEO of a company you're applying to, what would you tell him or her to convince them that you're the best person for the job?

- For each job that you've held, which three things are you most proud of?

- Which skills would your current and former coworkers say you're exceptionally good at?

- What kinds of awards and recognition have you received?

- When have you gone above and beyond the line of duty to accomplish something great?

- If you were packaged as an action figure and put on a shelf in a "job candidate store", how would you position yourself to stand out from the other action figures and make the recruiter want to buy you?

- Picture a former manager on the phone with a recruiter giving you a positive reference—what reasons would they be giving for why you'd be a great fit for the role?

You don't have to limit yourself to only using these questions to formulate your content, but they can help you jumpstart your thought process and get the gears turning. Outlining your achievements this way before building your formal resume will remove tremendous pressure from the process because you won't be expecting to come away with something perfect right off the bat. You should view this process as if you're carving your resume from a block of stone—it won't look like much at first, but by the time you're done, it will be a polished masterpiece. And like any masterpiece, it requires thorough preparation and planning to bring to life.

Only when you've completed the planning process and are satisfied that you've adequately captured your most impressive accomplishments should you start building your formal resume structure. The planning process can take a few hours, especially if you're building your resume from scratch, so be honest with yourself and don't shortchange it. Assuming that you've put the appropriate amount of time and thought into preparation, it's time to begin constructing the framework within which your accomplishments will reside.

CHAPTER 5

RESUME FORMATTING AND STYLING

This chapter covers a lot of ground with regards to style and formatting, so before we dive in it's important to provide some perspective. For that, we have Resume Golden Rule #3:

RESUME GOLDEN RULE #3

Stand out with substance, not with style.

At the end of the day, your accomplishments and fit for the role will be what get you hired, not how pretty your words look on the page. Now, don't get me wrong—your resume still needs to be clean and mistake-free in order to stay in the good graces of your target audience. However, you can't use style to compensate for a lack of substance, as recruiters will see through that from a mile away.

The story below offers a real-life example of what can happen if you rely too heavily on style to do the work for you.

The cautionary tale of Nina and Airbnb

In 2015, a young woman named Nina had one goal: to land a job at Airbnb. She tried to contact Airbnb multiple times to discuss going to work there, but wasn't able to capture anyone's interest. Discouraged but undeterred, she set out to create something that would be impossible for the company to ignore: an elaborate, beautifully designed resume that looked like it had been created by Airbnb itself. It even had its own website: www.nina4airbnb.com.

After spending an entire week on the project, she revealed it to the world—and generated a firestorm of attention. It racked up nearly half a million hits before catching the attention of CEO Brian Chesky himself, who tweeted, "I am reviewing right now. Very impressive."

Unfortunately for Nina, the company ultimately decided that she wasn't the right fit for the role. And while her out-of-the-box approach sparked conversations with other high profile tech companies, it ultimately failed to achieve her goal of becoming an Airbnb employee.

The lesson is simple: all the style in the world can't make up for a lack of whatever your target company is looking for. Ignoring substance in favor of style is a move you make at your own peril. By sticking to the fundamentals, you'll be much better positioned to invest your time where it counts and achieve the outcome you're aiming for.[6] [7] [8]

Page Length

One of the things recruiters will be judging you on is your ability to be succinct, and nothing says the opposite more than a rambling, unnecessarily long resume. With that in mind, it's time to introduce Golden Rule Number Four:

RESUME GOLDEN RULE #4

Your resume should be exactly one page long (except in rare circumstances).

Some people might find this advice controversial, but they're usually the people being paid to write resumes by the page. Unless you're in a highly technical field or a twenty-plus year industry veteran, keep your resume to just a single page (and even in those cases it may be questionable).

In case you've forgotten, recruiters are overwhelmed by the sheer number of resumes they process on a daily basis, so they need to handle them as efficiently as possible. A resume that's over a page in length presents them with all kinds of hassles like having to staple the printed pages together for distribution to other team members and scrolling to the next page to see things at the bottom like awards and education. It may sound unfair, but if your resume is over a page in length, recruiters will place a higher burden of proof on you to demonstrate your excellence in order to justify doubling their resume processing time. And if it fails to deliver? Well, let's just say that's an impression you don't want to make.

Another reason it's important to keep your resume to a single page is that it forces you to exercise extremely high standards toward what you choose to include. Operating within this constraint will ensure that only the best, most impressive content ends up in the final version. It's easy to just list everything you've ever done and slap it into a Word document that ends up being two or three pages long, but that practically guarantees two to three pages of mediocrity that a recruiter will be quick to pass over. A single page of highly concentrated awesomeness will beat out multiple pages of diluted, uninspired drivel any day of the week.

Content Density and Margins

The content of your resume should be laid out in a logical structure with the words striking a proper balance with the white space on the page. The last thing a recruiter wants to be confronted with is a continuous block of text. On the contrary, if the content of your resume only fills up half the page, the recruiter will think your resume is too light. There's a Goldilocks balance to be struck here, and the rule is this:

> **Your resume should always extend to the bottom of the page (with proper margins), and you should aim for a content density between 30 and 50%.**

The Golden Rule for page length is that the resume should fit one page *exactly*, not "*up to*" one page. This is important because it helps your resume pass the scan test, and appearing too light or too heavy could reduce your resume's effectiveness. Applying the appropriate level of content density helps to ensure that this doesn't happen to your resume.

Content density refers to the proportion of words and other characters on the page to the amount of whitespace on the page. Too much content, and the recruiter will be overwhelmed. Too little, and they'll view your resume as being light on qualifications.

A content density of 50% means that if your resume content began in the upper lefthand corner of the page, with zero margins, and flowed continuously across the page with no formatting, the content would end right at the middle of the page.

To illustrate, here are depictions of different levels of content density, with the black areas representing resume content:

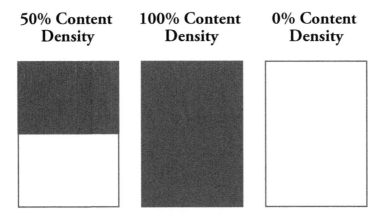

50% Content Density   **100% Content Density**   **0% Content Density**

Adjusting the page margins is the easiest way to modify the content density up or down depending on how much content you have. One inch margins will fill 37% of the surface area of an 8.5" x 11" sheet of paper with white space, so that may be a good option if you're fairly light on content. If you're struggling to fit all the content onto a single page, bringing the margins down to 0.5" will start you off with only 20% of the surface area taken up by white space. Just remember not to trim the margins so much that they push your content beyond the print boundary.

1" margins =	0.5" margins =
37% White Space	**20% White Space**

37% for margins		20% for margins	
	63% for content		**80% for content**

If you need to trim your margins to accommodate a lot of content, it's usually best to employ wider margins at the top and bottom of the page (at the very least, the top) than on the sides as having too little space between your first block of content and the upper edge of the page can make the resume feel cramped. So, if you reduce the left and right margins to 0.5", for example, adjust the top margin to 1".

Finding the proper balance between content and white space is more art than science, but it's not something you need to stress over. One method to quickly assess your content density is to print out your resume and let your eyes unfocus so that the content appears slightly blurred (kind of like you may have done with those Magic Eye[9] 3D image books they used to make). Is the page filled with too much text? Or does it seem like there's far more whitespace than content, making the resume look too light? This exercise should give you a pretty good idea, but if you still have questions you can always have a friend or family member look it over for you.

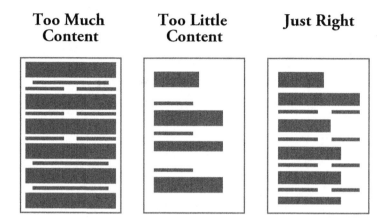

| Too Much Content | Too Little Content | Just Right |

Layout

When laying out the components of your resume, you need to keep Golden Rule Number Five in mind, which I alluded to previously:

RESUME GOLDEN RULE #5

Build your resume first to be scanned, then to be read.

Eye tracking studies have shown that recruiters only spend 6 seconds reviewing a resume[10], so that's how long you have to communicate the key information they're looking for and strike a good impression. In the span of those 6 seconds, they'll be looking for four specific pieces of information:

- Your name
- Your current position: job title, company, and dates of employment
- Your previous position: job title, company, and dates of employment
- Your education

Your resume is not the place to express your creativity, as Nina's story above illustrates. Regardless of how much you may find the restrictions of the traditional resume format stifling, companies and recruiters still engineer their workflows and hire people around it. Deviating from the traditional format poses an unnecessary risk and dramatically raises the bar for the qualifications you'll need to convey in order to justify the creative departure. So unless you're Mark Zuckerberg (and if you are—time for me to short Facebook stock!), stick to the basics and don't give the recruiter another reason to stick your resume in the rejection pile. The few extra seconds they'll spend trying to decipher your creative format could be reason enough for them to do so.

Font Style

Your tools for creating a killer resume lie in the elements of typography listed below. Used well, the combined elements come together in a beautiful symphony which invokes a sense of poise and competence in the reader. Used poorly, these elements may just leave the recruiter second-guessing the future of humanity (ok, that last part may be a slight exaggeration). The tools are:

- Font style (Arial, Times New Roman, etc.)
- Font size
- Font emphasis (bold, italics, etc.)
- Organizational elements (bullets, horizontal dividers, etc.)
- Spacing

The font style should be consistent throughout your entire resume or you'll risk looking careless or confusing the recruiter. It doesn't really matter which font you choose (except for Comic Sans, god forbid), as long as the information on your resume is clear and exudes professionalism. It's generally a good idea to pull from a handful of safe options which I've listed below:

Serif Fonts			
Garamond	Georgia	Cambria	Times New Roman
Sans-serif Fonts			
Helvetica	Calibri	Trebuchet MS	Arial
Verdana	Tahoma		

Serif fonts are those that have tiny decorative accents and are commonly used in book publishing. These fonts are especially useful for conveying the following characteristics:

- Traditional
- Stable
- Conservative
- Capable
- Classic

If you're applying for a job in a more conservative industry such as finance, using a serif font may be a safer option.

Sans-serif fonts do not contain the decorative accents that serif fonts do and evoke a more modern feel. Some traits that sans-serif fonts communicate are:

- Modern
- Crisp
- Innovative
- Clean
- Simple

If you're applying for a position in a more forward looking field such as technology or marketing, a sans-serif font may be better suited for your resume.

Another thing to consider with your font choice is how much space it takes up on the page. Some fonts, such as Garamond and Calibri, are more compact. Some, like Verdana and

Georgia, extend further than others for the same set of words. The table below illustrates the character density of the most commonly used resume fonts which all have the same font size:

Serif

The quick brown fox jumps over the lazy dog.	Garamond
The quick brown fox jumps over the lazy dog.	Georgia
The quick brown fox jumps over the lazy dog.	Cambria
The quick brown fox jumps over the lazy dog.	Times New Roman

Sans-serif

The quick brown fox jumps over the lazy dog.	Helvetica
The quick brown fox jumps over the lazy dog.	Calibri
The quick brown fox jumps over the lazy dog.	Trebuchet MS
The quick brown fox jumps over the lazy dog.	Arial
The quick brown fox jumps over the lazy dog.	Verdana
The quick brown fox jumps over the lazy dog.	Tahoma

In addition to page margins, your font choice can be a good lever to pull if you need to adjust your content density up or down. The differences between the fonts don't look like much in the above table, but when you have a page full of resume content they can easily add or take away almost a quarter of a page. Be careful not to go overboard with this, however—a resume with one inch margins and Verdana font may come dangerously close to looking too thin.

A word of warning regarding light fonts

Modern design has recently gravitated toward the use of light and ultra-light fonts, which do a good job of conveying elegance and modernity. The problem with these fonts is that they can make it more difficult for readers to read and comprehend the meaning of the words on a page. A 2016 eyetracking study[11] confirmed that the use of light and ultra-light fonts not only reduce legibility, but increase the reader's cognitive load as well. This presents a problem, because the last thing you want to do is make it harder for a recruiter to get through your resume.

Read the sentences below to get a sense of how the eyes strain to pick out the word flow and meaning in light font styles:

Compare the difficulty of getting through this sentence

With the relative ease of getting through this one.

An entire page consisting of a light font like the one used above will be especially tough to get through. If you decide to go outside the font "safe zone", be sure not to choose a font that's too light.

Pay particular attention to fonts with the words "New" or "Neue" in the names, as these tend to be lighter spinoffs of traditional fonts.

Font Size and Emphasis

Using a smart combination of font size and emphasis throughout your resume will call attention to the areas recruiters care about most and provide the logical structure they're looking for. Your use of headings, subheadings and other text elements should be consistent and easy for the recruiter to follow. You should assign the following pieces of information their own distinct font size and emphasis to make them easier to discern on the page:

Name

Your name should be the most prominent visual element on your resume and located at the top of the page. This is the first thing the recruiter's eyes will be drawn to when she starts to scan your resume, so it should be bold and convey a sense of confidence and capability. This is your personal brand after all—make the recruiter excited to learn more about what you bring to the table!

As a general rule, the font size you use for your name should be at least two points higher than the next largest font on the page. So, if you're using 14 point font for your headings, then your name should be at least 16 point. If you still want to make your name more prominent, you can use bold and/ or all caps. I personally display my name in bold *and* all caps to give it an extra dose of gravitas.

Headings

Headings are used to distinguish major sections of your resume like professional experience, education, skills and activities, and awards. These should be the most prominent visual elements on the page aside from your name. A good guideline to follow is to make your heading sizes two points larger than the rest of your resume content (excluding your name, which will be the largest). So if the bullets under your headings are 12 point font, your headings would be 14 point. Then, apply bold, caps, and/or italics to make them more prominent.

Subheadings

Subheadings are used to call out the important information contained under your section headings, like company names, job titles, employment dates, schools attended, etc. These should have the same font size as the rest of the body content with either bold or italics for emphasis. You should be consistent with your use of subheadings throughout your resume so the recruiter can easily discern the information contained within. For instance, if you decide to use bold for company names under the professional experience heading, then you should use bold for school names under the education heading as well.

Here's an illustration of the font size principles mentioned above:

Font Size		
20 pt.	**JOE SMITH**	Name
14 pt.	*PROFESSIONAL EXPERIENCE*	Heading
12 pt.	**Company, Inc.**	Subheading

Section Heading Alignment

Assuming your resume is in English, recruiters will be reading it from left to right. You want to make it as easy as possible for the recruiter to scan your resume for critical information, so left-justifying your section headings is usually the way to go. Center-justifying your section headings adds a block of whitespace between the left margin of the page and the section heading, which takes a fraction of a second longer for the eye to get to than left-justified headings. Center-justifying also creates the need to add emphasis or horizontal dividers to make it easier for the recruiter to discern between sections, which can make your resume look too busy. Your best bet is to play it safe and left-justify your section headings.

Center Justified   **Left Justified**

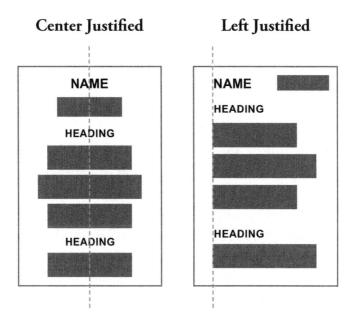

A Word About Underlines

My thought on underlines is that they have no place on a resume because they make them look too busy. Every time I've seen a resume using underlines to draw emphasis, it's appeared much too cluttered. You can accomplish everything you need to from a formatting perspective using font size, bold, italics, and caps and your resume will look much cleaner. Using horizontal dividers can be okay (to separate your name from the rest of the resume, for instance), but use with care. A good rule of thumb is "when in doubt, leave it out." Err on the side of simplicity and you won't have to worry about your resume looking too busy.

The vertical bar: Your best friend for content layout

If you have a lot of content to fit onto your resume, you may not be able to stack information like company name, job title, and dates of employment on top of each other without causing the content to flow onto another page. Enter the vertical bar, or pipe. This character (|) can be used to condense this information into a single line, leaving more room for bullets and other information. Using a vertical bar, we can go from this:

Shell Oil Company
Account Manager
Houston, TX

To this:

Shell Oil Company | *Account Manager* | Houston, TX

You'll still want to maintain the font emphasis to call out the individual elements of the position, but in this case using the vertical bar frees up another two lines for information.

Alternatively, you can use a hyphen to find middle ground between the original version and the condensed version using a vertical bar, as shown below:

Shell Oil Company - Houston, TX
Account Manager

Whichever method you choose, make sure you use it consistently throughout your entire resume!

Color

There are competing fields of thought on the use of color in a resume, but my view is that it's best to leave color out. There's a good chance that if your resume is printed, it will be printed in black and white as this is the default color mode for a lot of printers. A rule of thumb here is that your resume should stand on its own without the addition of any color. It should pass the copy test: If this resume were copied in black and white, would it be just as easy to discern the important parts of it as it is in color? The marginal benefits of adding color to a resume are slight if any, so you're better off not worrying about it.

Line Spacing

You should aim for line spacing between 1.0 and 1.15. Anything lower and your resume will feel too cluttered, and anything higher and your resume will feel too light.

Ratcheting up the line spacing may have been a quick way to pad the contents of a research paper in high school (come on, don't act like you don't know what I'm talking about!), but it has no place in a resume. Recruiters will instantly think less of your qualifications if there's too much spacing and your content feels light.

 To see real-world examples of resumes that meet these formatting and style criteria, download my five free resume templates by visiting www.danclay.com/perfectresume.

CHAPTER 6

THE MEAT AND POTATOES: YOUR RESUME CONTENT

Flow

In the six seconds a recruiter spends scanning your resume, they should be able to pull every piece of information they're looking for without getting lost in the layout. Recruiters have come to expect the following flow of information in a resume, from top to bottom:

1. Name and contact information (required)

2. Profile or summary (optional)

3. Work Experience (required)

4. Other Activities (charity work, membership in organizations, etc) (optional)

5. Awards (optional)

6. Skills/Certifications (optional)

7. Education (required)

Your job with every section is to make a strong enough impression to entice the reader to move on to the next section. Any weak links could be cause for abandonment, so it's important you make your resume airtight.

Voice

A strong voice is key to carrying a strong resume. So key, in fact, that it warrants another Golden Rule:

RESUME GOLDEN RULE #6

Use an active voice to communicate the accomplishments on your resume.

Write your resume with words that convey action and conviction, not modesty or timidity. Of course, you shouldn't overtly brag about your achievements, but recruiters expect you to toot your own horn when you're talking about what you've accomplished. You'll impress the recruiter by being tactful, professional, and confident.

When writing your resume, use an active voice as opposed to a passive voice. Writing in an active voice evokes a sense of energy and momentum that passive voice lacks. Let's look at how dramatically different a situation can sound when phrased in an active versus a passive voice:

Active voice:

> The driver slammed the car into the median, sending shards of glass and metal everywhere.

Passive voice:

> The car was damaged in an accident on the freeway.

It's not hard to pick out the sentence that conveys the most energy, is it? Your resume should generate a similar sense of excitement and action that makes the recruiter want to pick up the phone and call you for an interview right then and there (without summoning the emotions associated with a car accident, of course!).

The "Hell Yea!" Test

When you're writing the different sections of your resume, use the "Hell Yea!" test to judge whether or not your voice is strong enough. After you're finished writing a section, re-read it and ask yourself: "does this make me want to say 'Hell Yea!' after reading it?" If not, try to rephrase things using a more energetic voice. Here's an example of a sentence from the executive summary section of a resume that goes from failing the "Hell Yea!" test to passing it with flying colors:

Not Bad:

> Skilled negotiator with experience managing complex relationships and executing high-value contracts that makes me a leader among my peers.

Hell Yea!:

> Masterfully negotiate complex, multimillion-dollar contracts and consistently place in the top 10% of target performance among my peers.

See the difference? Active voice should carry your resume from top to bottom and communicate your achievements in the most impressive way possible without lying or sounding pretentious. Make your reader *feel* the greatness oozing from the page. Your resume has to sell the reader on your capabilities without you being there to explain yourself, so treat every word as an opportunity to do so.

A key difference that can help you identify active versus passive voice is that passive voice tends to communicate things you *are*, while active voice generally communicates things you *do*. In the above example, "Skilled negotiator" is a passive way of describing the person's characteristics. Rephrasing the noun "negotiator" to the verb "negotiate" brings to life the person's characteristics into a concrete action that communicates more and sounds better at the same time. To maintain a consistent active voice, express your achievements using verbs and adverbs rather than adjectives and nouns whenever possible. This will inject the high energy needed to carry the reader from the top to the bottom of the page and get them excited to learn more about you in person or over the phone.

Nailing this voice consistently throughout your resume is admittedly tricky. To help you get on the right track, I've made a resource available for free titled **77 Hard-Hitting Resume Action Verbs and Phrase Examples** that you can download by visiting www.danclay.com/perfectresume. In it, you'll find a collection of high-energy verbs put into the context of how they might appear on a resume. Feel free to copy and paste to your heart's delight—just make sure to update the figures to be an accurate representation of your achievements!

Key Resume Areas

NAME AND CONTACT INFORMATION

Your name and contact information will be the first things a recruiter sees when he picks up your resume, so it's important to organize this information in a clean manner to make a positive first impression.

Include the following in this section:

Name

The name you display on your resume should match the name on your LinkedIn profile, as recruiters will often look you up as part of the vetting process. It's generally best to use your full birth name as opposed to a nickname as it will be easier for the recruiter to cross-reference this information once they get to the background check stage, but do whatever's most comfortable for you. If your full name is difficult to pronounce or all of your online profiles use a nickname, stick with the nickname. It's also your choice whether or not to include your middle name or middle initial. Doing so can add a nice formal touch but it doesn't really make a difference one way or the other.

Email address

Keep it professional, but make sure not to tie it to the email address of your current employer. If you end up leaving your current job, you'll lose access to everything tied to your work email, which presents a problem if you've been using your work email to communicate with your new employer and keep track of things like contact information, offer letters, and other employment documents.

If you're applying for a position in a forward-looking field like technology or marketing, make sure your email address is from a modern provider such as Gmail and not from providers that are considered antiquated like AOL or Juno. Gmail accounts are free and easy to obtain, so if you have to, get a new email address just for your resume.

Ready for a shock? A whopping *seventy-six percent* of resumes are discarded for having an unprofessional email address[12], so keep the born2Bw1ld@ or QTpie69@ email addresses between friends only! The email address you use to represent your professional identity should be some variation of your name to convey the tone of professionalism that companies desire. If tom.smith@ is taken, for example, don't sweat it—something like tom.j.smith@ or tom.smith24@ would be fine.

Phone Number

You should only include one phone number on your resume for the phone that you're most accessible to during normal business hours—excluding your work phone. You don't want to run into the awkward situation of receiving a call from a recruiter on your work line and having to tell them in a hushed tone that you'll call them back in a few minutes. For most people, their personal cell number is the best one for their resume. In terms of format, simple and elegant works best. Using periods to separate the area code and number blocks can be a nice professional touch:

From this:

> ➜ (220) 978-4408

To this:

> ➜ 220.978.4408

Physical address

It's standard to include the street, city, state and zip of the address you'll be spending the majority of your time in during the interview process. If you're applying for a role while in college, for example, you should include your school address rather than that of your parents. Don't put more than one address on the resume, either, as this will take up unnecessary space and confuse the recruiter. It's also acceptable to only include the city and state abbreviation (e.g. "San Diego, CA") to convey a more minimalist look.

A Word on Labels

It's best to leave out labels such as "Phone", "Email", etc. as these are implied and add unnecessary clutter.

So, rather than displaying this:

→ **Email:** tom.smith@gmail.com

You'd simply display this:

→ tom.smith@gmail.com

How should you display your address if you're applying to a position that would require relocating?

All qualifications equal, most companies would prefer to hire a local candidate than to have to pay to relocate someone from another state or country. The obvious downside to this is that it can limit the pool of open positions to which you can apply. If you're applying to a role out of state, you may be tempted to lie on your resume and include an address that matches the location of the role you're applying for.

This is a mistake!

Doing so may land you an initial phone screen, but once the in-person interviews begin there are a bunch of things that could go wrong. For one, recruiters are notorious for switching interview dates at the last second—do you really want to pay for your own flight to an interview only to find out that it's been moved to the following week? And if you do well, there's also a chance that they'll call you back in to meet with other members of the team which means another flight on your dime. Finally, if they do find out you're not local, you'll lose credibility and potentially be rejected from the candidate pool for your dishonesty.

The best policy with your address and any other item on your resume is to be upfront and honest with the information you provide. This will protect your professional integrity and get your relationship with your potential employer off on the right foot. Some companies just don't hire candidates from out of state, so you'd rather find that out earlier than after you've potentially invested days of your time into the interview process. If you are willing to relocate for the position, you can include "Open to relocation" next to your current address.

PROFILE/EXECUTIVE SUMMARY

Including a brief summary of your skills and qualifications can help the recruiter quickly assess your suitability for the role. Think of this as your "elevator pitch"—you want to paint a picture of your professional credentials that will make the recruiter eager to scan further down the page. This section shouldn't take up any more than four or five lines, otherwise you'll risk losing the recruiter before they move on to your professional experience.

It's important to tie this summary to the role you're specifically applying for and include keywords that will help your resume pass the ATS filter. For instance, if you're applying for a Data Analyst role with a requirement listed in the job description to "Work collaboratively with all teams to deliver actionable insights into our product to further increase user acquisition, engagement, and monetization", you might say:

> "Highly adept at analyzing large data sets from multiple sources to determine ongoing product strategy driving customer acquisition."

This is one of the toughest sections of the resume to write because you only have a few sentences in which to highlight the most important attributes you think will catch the recruiter's attention. Plus, you may need to customize this for each role you're applying for if there are significant differences in requirements.

Should you include an objective in your resume?

To put it simply: No. Recruiters know your objective is to be hired into the role you're applying for, so there's no sense wasting valuable resume real estate on something so obvious. Plus, who cares what *you* want (no offense)? You're selling yourself on the value you'll bring to their company, not telling them what you want and hoping they can give it to you. Keep your content focused on the unique capabilities and experience you bring to the table and why they should invite you to interview for the role. Think "what's in it for them?"—that's what the recruiter will be thinking as they scan your resume.

PROFESSIONAL EXPERIENCE

The professional experience section of your resume is the one that the recruiter will be paying the most attention to. It's crucial that you use strong, energetic language to highlight your unique capabilities and sell yourself for the role. I prefer using the term "Professional Experience" over "Work Experience" as the latter comes off slightly less polished.

Your professional experience should be listed in reverse chronological order with your most recent place of employment at the top. Include the company name, your title, location where you worked, and dates of employment in that position. This information shouldn't take up more than two lines, and each component should be distinctly identified in a consistent manner using font emphasis. Bold text tends to draw the eyes' attention, so it's good form to use it for information like this that the recruiter will be specifically looking for. A solid best practice is to accent the company names and dates of employment in bold and the role titles in italics, like so:

Google, Inc. - Mountain View, CA   **March 2013 - May 2015**
Partnerships Manager

Remember, the name of the game when it comes to formatting is *consistency*, so pay attention to the little things. Don't write the month of December as "Dec." in some places and "December" in others, for instance. Make sure your sentences are punctuated correctly with proper grammar and spelling.

Underneath the position information, list your most impressive accomplishments in bullets, not paragraphs. It's much easier for a recruiter to quickly gather this information when it's in bullet format than it is for them to read through a block of text. When listing your achievements across multiple positions, use the "5 For 5" rule:

If you held the position within the past five years, shoot for five bullets max per position. If you held the position more than five years ago, you're only allowed three bullets max.

You don't need to apply this rule as strictly if you've only held one or two positions and require more bullets for each position to fill out your resume content—just make sure the additional accomplishments you highlight are relevant to the job description and that they carry the momentum you've established in previous bullets.

Because recruiters put less weight on your professional experience the further back you go in your work history, it's better to highlight more information from your recent employment experiences than from older ones. Plus, during your interview you'll get more questions about your recent work experience which you'll be able to speak to more accurately because they'll be fresh in your mind.

In fact, I'd recommend leaving off any work experience that took place over fifteen years ago, with the exception being if the position is your current role OR the experience is more relevant to the position you're applying to than your more recent experience . It becomes difficult to hold your resume to one page if you include jobs from that far back in your career, and unless they're particularly relevant to the role you're applying for they can do more harm than good. If you're considered more tenured in your career, this information can betray your age and cause the recruiter to pass you up before they call you for an interview. Technically this is illegal, but there's no way to prove it if they never contact you in the first place. Don't take that chance.

How you communicate your accomplishments is critical for making your resume stand out above the rest. Introducing Golden Rule Number Seven:

RESUME GOLDEN RULE #7

Describe your accomplishments in terms of results, not responsibilities.

The following framework comes in handy when you're thinking about how to construct the bullets for your resume. Your bullets should generally meet the following three criteria, which when combined come together to form the Three R Model for Bullet Building:

The Three R Model for Bullet Building:

- Relevant
- Relative
- Results-oriented

The first criteria your bullets must meet is that of relevance to the job to which you're applying. It's crucial to align the results you communicate to the listed responsibilities for the role in order to get past the ATS filter (remember the keyword test?). If one of the stated responsibilities is to "**Retain** and **grow** revenue with our largest **mid-market** partners", for example, your bullet may look like this (common words in bold):

- Drove 85% client **retention** for a book of 37 **mid-market** accounts and surpassed account **growth** targets by 55% in 2014.

Not every bullet on your resume has to directly align with a specific keyword or set of keywords mentioned in the job description, but the majority should. You should also list the bullets under each position of professional experience in order of most relevant to least relevant. Often, recruiters will only read the first one or two bullets at first glance, so it's best to lead with those that most closely match the keywords or main themes pulled from the job description.

To help figure out the order in which to list your bullets, you can start by asking yourself, "if I could only show the recruiter one bullet, which one would it be?" Make that your first bullet. Then, continue to ask yourself the same question with the remaining bullets until all are accounted for on your resume.

The second test your bullets must pass, relativity, refers to how your results stand up to a standard measure of performance. For instance, simply saying "Sold $5 million contract value in 2015" doesn't mean much on its own. Is that a lot? A little? You want to compare your performance to established targets or peer averages whenever possible to give the recruiter a sense of the magnitude of your achievements.

So, you might say something like "Achieved 150% of target contract value sales with $5 million sold in 2015."

When it comes to bullets on a resume, the more quantifiable they are, the better. Try to think of ways to articulate your achievements into tangible value statements that will resonate immediately with the recruiter.

For example, say you led a project which streamlined the workflow for a process inside your company. How much time did that save for each person involved in the process? How much are those people paid and what is that time worth?

You can figure out the math like so in the following hypothetical example:

- 8 people
- Approximately 2 hours saved each per week
- Approx. $60,000/year salaries for each
- 50 weeks/year x 40 hours/week = 2,000 hours worked per year for each
- $60,000/2,000 hours = $30/hr
- $30/hr x 2 hours/week saved x 8 people = $480/week
- $480/week x 52 weeks/year = $25,000/year

This technique is known as framing, and it's especially useful for making your results sound more impressive without having to lie about them. In the above example, reframing the benefit from a time savings to a dollar savings and from a weekly amount to an annual amount makes the figure both easier to understand and more significant to the reader. If you're unsure of the specific numbers involved, take an educated guess—just be sure you're able to confidently talk through how you arrived at your numbers during an interview. You can pull quick salary estimates for any position from Glassdoor.com to keep your numbers as grounded in reality as possible.

It goes without saying, but I'll say it anyway: don't over-inflate your achievements beyond a reasonable level just to make them sound more impressive. The more extraordinary they sound, the more recruiters and interviewers will ask you for greater detail about them, and you may find yourself in a position of digging a deeper hole of lies. The truth has a way of coming out eventually, and the last thing you want is for an opportunity to be yanked out from under you right when it's within your grasp. If you've never heard the story[13] of former Yahoo.com CEO Scott Thompson, give it a read— you don't want that to happen to you, trust me.

Finally, your bullets must focus on results, not responsibilities. Just by applying for the role, the recruiter will assume that you meet its basic requirements, so she'll be looking for evidence that you'd excel in the role rather than just meet expectations. You'll need to highlight achievements from your experience that make you stand out and give the recruiter a sense of how you'd handle the role you're applying for.

The impact of constructing your
bullets around results rather than
responsibilities is perhaps best illustrated
by a real-life example of a resume
that's been transformed from one
focusing on responsibilities to one
focusing on results. See for yourself
by downloading the **Resume Before
and After Transformation** example at
www.danclay.com/perfectresume.

*Should you include a description of each
company under your professional experience?*

Some people include a brief description of
each company directly under the employment
information, but in my opinion it's best to leave
this off. If you've caught the attention of a recruiter
and they haven't heard of a company listed in your
experience, they'll do their own research and look
it up on Google or LinkedIn. And if the company
is well-known, including a description of what
they do will be an insult to their intelligence. Your
accomplishments will largely be what matter most
to a recruiter, not where you achieved them (unless
it was at a top-tier company—you'll get extra

points for that). Taking up a line or two of resume real estate to describe something the recruiter can find for himself does a disservice to the capabilities you're trying to communicate. Use that space for your results bullets instead!

Displaying multiple roles held at the same company

Holding multiple roles at the same company is a positive indicator of forward advancement and showcases your willingness to try new things without leaving the organization. If you've held multiple consecutive roles within the same company, it's best to display the company name and dates of employment across those roles as a heading, then the different titles you've held along with the specific timeframes and bulleted results for each.

Here's an example:

Google, Inc. - Mountain View, CA   **Feb. 2011 - May 2015**

Partnerships Manager (May 2013 - May 2015)
 • Bullet 1
 • Bullet 2
 • Bullet 3

Business Development Associate (Feb. 2011 - April 2013)
 • Bullet 1
 • Bullet 2
 • Bullet 3

If you've held multiple roles at the same company but worked at one or more companies in between those roles, list them as you would normally in reverse chronological order. Otherwise, it will be more difficult for the recruiter to follow your work history.

Communicating Acquisitions

If your previous employer was acquired by your current employer and you still hold the same role that you held when the company was acquired, you'll want to note that on your resume to indicate that you landed at the company by means of an acquisition. A simple statement in parentheses is sufficient, like so:

LinkedIn Corp (Acquired Bizo Inc. July 2014)   **Dec. 2013 - Present**
Product Manager

If you've moved on to another role in the company since the acquisition, you'll want to separate the roles and display the acquisition in a slightly different manner:

LinkedIn Corp	**Oct. 2015 - Present**
Sr. Product Director	
......	
Bizo Inc (Acquired by LinkedIn July 2014)	**Dec. 2013 - Sept. 2015**
Product Manager	

Displaying the acquired company as a separate entity in this case makes it easier for the recruiter to quickly discern the progression of your career path. As a rule of thumb, you should only have one set of bullets per position held, so it wouldn't make sense to have a different set of bullets for the same position you held at both the acquired company and your new company.

Explaining Gaps In Your Resume

If you haven't been employed in over six months, you should provide further explanation for this gap on your resume. Many people fret over such gaps, but if they were taken for the right reasons these gaps can actually have a positive effect and separate you from the pack.

I have a friend who quit his job and traveled around Southeast Asia for a year before returning to the States and finding a higher paying job than the one he had left. Other people leave in pursuit of starting a business or immersing themselves in something they're passionate about before returning to work full time. As long as you can point to the gap as an area of self development that has helped you become a more well-rounded person, it will generally be regarded in a positive light. Who hasn't wanted to drop everything and travel the world for a few months? The fact that you did will set you apart as someone who can contribute a unique perspective to the company.

Here's how you could display two examples of employment gaps in a way that positions you positively:

World Traveler   **June 2015 - April 2016**
Pursued my passion for experiencing unique cultures by exploring 17 different countries in Asia, Europe, and South America.

Who wouldn't want to talk to you with that kind of life experience? Some recruiters would probably want to set up a phone interview just to ask you how to do the same

There's no shame in highlighting a business you may have started that didn't achieve the level of success you had hoped for. The fact that you took the risk to pursue something you're passionate about sets you apart from the millions of people who never will. Plus, companies love people who have experience hustling to run a small business.

If you haven't held a job in over six months and haven't done anything but sit around and play video games the entire time, the gap will be significantly harder to explain. Companies are looking to hire people who still hold that professional edge that makes them effective in the workplace, and the longer you go without working, the softer you'll get and the more difficult it will be to land a job with a company you want to work for. The best thing you can do during these employment gaps is to continue developing your skills and demonstrate that you're more than capable of jumping back into the workplace. If you're not sure how to start a business, start by launching a blog. Create something you can point your interviewer to that showcases your passion and creativity. Learn a new skill, a new language, or build your knowledge of something you've always been interested in.

To get the job you want, you first have to earn it—and you do this by demonstrating the traits the company is looking for. They don't want someone who's lazy, entitled, and unwilling to learn anything new. They want someone who's passionate, always looking to expand beyond their comfort zones, and eager to take on challenges as they come their way. If you don't fall into the latter group, there's no better time to start than now!

Displaying Dates on Your Resume

When it comes to formatting dates on your resume, you have two options: numerical (i.e. 8/2011) and alphabetical (i.e. August 2011). In my opinion, you should always spell out the names of the months on your resume in order to make the timeframes of your experience more clear to the recruiter. Having to mentally translate an "8" into "August" is just one more mental step the recruiter has to take in their frenetic resume review process. If you find yourself running low on space, it's safe to abbreviate the names of the months (i.e. Jan.), just make sure that you're consistent in your abbreviations throughout your resume. You don't want to display one month as "Jan." and another as "January" further down your resume, as this will look sloppy.

Also, you'll want to create some space between the dates to avoid making them look too cluttered. By adding a single space before and after each hyphen in your date ranges, you'll make the text much easier to read. Here's an example:

Too Tight:

→ Dec. 2011-May 2012

Just Right:

→ Dec. 2011 - May 2012

It's a small detail, but the little things add up. You can also separate dates with a "to" instead of a hyphen, like this:

Dec. 2011 to May 2012

If I had to choose one over the other, I'd say the hyphenated format is a better choice because it looks less cluttered and gives the recruiter one less word to read.

Should you include jobs you only held for a brief period of time?

Reliability is one of the qualities recruiters will be looking for in an ideal candidate, so if you've held any positions for less than six months it might make sense to leave them off. There are a couple of exceptions here, though.

First, if the position was seasonal, then the recruiter will expect you to have held it only during that time period and it won't be seen as a negative.

Secondly, if the position gave you valuable insights into what you want out of your career, then it can be safe to leave it on as a part of your personal narrative.

For instance, if you worked in banking for a few months before realizing that you hated it and took your career down a completely different path (like I did), you should absolutely include that in your story. Recruiters love seeing that you've learned something from your experiences and will generally view major career inflection points as a positive— just make sure that you're prepared to explain them in further detail if asked.

As long as your experience doesn't portray you as a perpetual job hopper, you should be fine. The last thing a recruiter wants is to invest a lot of time and resources into the hiring process only to have you leave after three months and put them back at square one. Unless you absolutely hate a particular job, it's best to stick it out for at least a year before looking for greener pastures.

PROFESSIONAL ACTIVITIES AND VOLUNTEER WORK

Activities outside of your day-to-day job can help position you in a more well-rounded light and show the recruiter what you're passionate about. Having a job is the most obvious area in which people choose to invest their time, and almost everybody needs one to pay the bills. Highlighting activities outside of work makes you immediately stand out from the majority of people who don't have them.

Typically, this section can be a catch-all for anything you may have pursued outside of a regular job. Did you start a company in college? Build houses for Habitat for Humanity? Start a club? You can include anything that demonstrates your leadership capabilities and initiative here, unless it could potentially harm your professional reputation. If you'd be uncomfortable discussing it with an interviewer, it's probably best to leave it off.

If you don't have much professional experience to include in your resume, you can supplement your lack of content in that area with more content highlighting your experience outside of work. This is common for many college graduates who haven't had a chance to hold positions relevant to the roles they're applying for. It's far better to include relevant experience from outside of work than to have a resume that doesn't fill the entire page.

Whether or not to include a section like this is a question only you can answer for yourself, but it's an important enough consideration to warrant its own Golden Rule:

RESUME GOLDEN RULE #8

Always prioritize the information that is most relevant to the role you're applying for.

Say you're applying for an entry-level finance position and you're running out of space on your resume. You can include either your recent experience as a Subway sandwich artist, or as the finance chair for your fraternity. Including the latter would mean creating a new section because the finance chair position isn't an actual job. What do you do?

It may seem obvious, but including your experience as the finance chair is the clear choice here because it more directly relates to the finance position you're applying for.

Should you include entry-level jobs unrelated to the role you're applying for?

Ideally, you shouldn't include any positions on your resume that don't demonstrate some kind of aptitude for the role you're applying for. However, every job you may have held likely has *something* you can highlight that the recruiter would find interesting. As long as you highlight results rather than responsibilities, it's possible to position your experience from even an entry-level job as a valuable asset to a company. Did you show forward advancement into more demanding positions? Were you looked at as a leader among other employees? Did you improve any processes or help your employer realize value as a result of your efforts? All of these convey the traits employers are looking for, regardless of the environment in which you demonstrated them.

You should only highlight entry-level roles on your resume if you're struggling to find content to fill it with. If you already have enough content to fill an entire page, then it's better to leave them off unless they're highly relevant to the role you're applying for, in which case you may want to think about including it and removing the less relevant experience.

SKILLS & CERTIFICATIONS

Dedicating an area of your resume to highlight particular skills or specialized training you possess can provide readers with additional information about your capabilities that wouldn't naturally fit anywhere else on your resume. Used properly, this section can provide valuable context for readers to assess your suitability for a particular role.

You should only include those skills that are both relevant to the role and those the recruiter won't reasonably assume you already have. These days, every employer will expect you to know how to use software like Microsoft Word, Excel, and PowerPoint at a basic proficiency level, so it's not necessary to explicitly mention them on your resume. However, if you possess anything more than basic proficiency with a common piece of software, you should absolutely highlight this to differentiate your skillset.

Use the following designations to indicate your skill level with a certain piece of software, in order of increasing proficiency:

- Intermediate
- Advanced
- Expert

There are no formal rules separating the designations, but the following guidelines can be helpful when considering how to position your level of expertise:

Intermediate: Top 50% expertise; you know how to do more with the software than 50% of people with at least a basic proficiency level.

Advanced: Top 75% expertise; you know how to do more with the software than 75% of people with at least a basic proficiency level. People come to you with questions and you're generally seen as a go-to resource.

Expert: Top 95% expertise; you know how to do more with the software than 95% of people with at least a basic proficiency level. You're recognized as a thought leader and have contributed to the ongoing development of the community.

Displaying these on your resume is fairly straightforward; simply list the software with the skill designation in parentheses in bullet form under the skills section and separate each piece of software with a comma. Putting each skill on a separate line is a bit overkill and will take up way too much space, so try to keep these to one bullet. The following provides an example:

SKILLS
- Adobe Web Analytics, Salesforce, Microsoft Excel (Advanced)

In the above example, because Adobe Analytics and Salesforce are not software programs that everybody would know how to use, it's acceptable to include them without a proficiency designation. However, if you hold more than a basic proficiency level with these or other non-universal software programs, you should include your designations where appropriate (as with Microsoft Excel above).

You should also include any certifications you hold as these will position you as more capable for the role. If your certification is prestigious and highly recognized in the industry, you should include it further up the resume to draw attention earlier as well as in its own designated section. For example, if you hold a Project Management Professional (PMP) certification, you may want to lead with this in the profile/executive summary section of your resume as well as include it in the Skills & Certifications section.

Here's an example of how this might look:

> **Profile**
> Certified Project Management Professional (PMP) with 9 years
> experience working in high technology....
> ......
> **Skills & Certifications**
> • Project Management Professional (PMP), 2011

Recruiters will understand what the certification means, so there's no need to elaborate any further beyond listing the certification name and the year you received it. If they're interested in discussing it further, they'll do so in the interview stage.

The Skills section is also the place to highlight any languages you may have proficiency in. There are four designations you can use to indicate your level of proficiency with a language:

- Basic
- Conversational
- Business
- Fluent

Like software proficiencies, there are no formal rules outlining how you characterize your level of mastery with a language. The following guidelines can help you position your proficiency, but if the recruiter really wants to clarify how comfortable you are with a language they'll be sure to ask.

Basic: You may be able to understand and speak decently well if you focus hard enough, but you'd have a hard time expressing and understanding ideas with someone who speaks the language fluently.

Conversational: You can hold an exchange with a fluent speaker for an extended period of time, and even though you may not understand every word being spoken you can grasp the fundamental concepts being communicated.

Business: You know the language well enough to conduct business in it and carry out instructions without error. You also have enough of an understanding of cultural idioms that you won't offend those who you do business with.

Fluent: You can carry an extended conversation with a native speaker at their own pace without skipping a beat.

Generally, employers will only care if you possess a business proficiency or higher with a language, as a lower proficiency level isn't practically useful for them. If you don't possess this level of proficiency with any language, it's probably best to leave the language part out. And no, you don't need to mention the fact that you're fluent in English when applying to predominantly English-speaking companies—that will be assumed from the language your resume is written in.

You should list any language proficiencies you have in a separate bullet within the Skills section, like so:

Skills & Certifications
- Project Management Professional (PMP), 2011
- Adobe Web Analytics, Salesforce, Microsoft Excel (Advanced)
- Languages: Spanish (Business), Arabic (Fluent)

If you possess a basic or conversational proficiency with a particular language, you don't need to include it unless it's specifically relevant to the role.

The title of this section, i.e. "Skills & Certifications", should reflect the content contained within. If you're only highlighting a set of certifications, shorten the title to simply say "Certifications". If you're listing a set of skills without formal certifications, the title should be "Skills". If you don't have any skills or certifications that are relevant to the role, then it's best not to include this section at all. There's no sense taking up space that would be better used for something more relevant.

Should you include a section just for keywords to help pass the ATS test?

Some advice floating around out there recommends that you create a separate section just for keywords to help you pass the ATS test. Nestled near the top of the resume under the Profile section and called something innocuous like "Proficiencies" or "Specialties", this section is designed specifically for the ATS filter under the guise of helping the recruiter better understand your capabilities without having to read further into your experience. Guess what? The recruiter won't be fooled—and you'll have wasted valuable resume real estate doing something that would have been better accomplished through the strategic wording of your bullets. Including a section just for keywords will do nothing except put the recruiter on high alert for someone who's looking to pad their resume, and that's not a position you want to put yourself in. As long as you put the necessary thought into wording your bullets correctly, you won't have to resort to cheap parlor tricks like keyword padding that are more likely to land your resume in the rejection pile than land you an interview.

EDUCATION

Your education should always appear at the bottom of your resume because that's where recruiters will be looking for it. Because most jobs require a minimum level of education, this section is one of the first things recruiters look for when they pick up your resume. It may seem like the top would be a good place for it, but because people include different types of information at the top, it's best to highlight it at the bottom where recruiters will be expecting it.

There's one exception, however: if you're applying for your first job out of college, then it's acceptable to include the education information at the top of your resume. Recruiters will understand that you likely won't have the breadth of professional experience that seasoned professionals do, so they won't penalize you for this.

As a rule of thumb, you should include every degree you've obtained in order of most advanced to least advanced, down to your Bachelor's degree. If you don't have a Bachelor's degree and aren't currently pursuing one, you should list any degree or diploma you've received from High School level or above. A high school education is the bare minimum that most employers that require a resume will accept, so don't include anything below that level.

The specific information you include in your education section should depend on how long it's been since you received the education. Generally speaking, employers care less about your academic pedigree and achievements the longer you've been out of school (unless you attended a top tier institution like an Ivy League). The following table provides some guidelines for which types of information you should include based on the amount of time since graduation:

Information	Include if
School name	Always
Degree type (B.A., B.S., etc)	Always
Major	Always
Minor	Always
Graduation year	Sometimes (optional if 15+ years since graduation)
Honors or distinctions	<5 years since graduation
GPA	<5 years since graduation and 3.5 or higher
Courses taken	Applying to first job after graduation
Scholarships	Applying to first job after graduation, unless extremely prestigious (e.g. Rhodes Scholar)

The more relevant your education to the role for which you're applying, the more you should emphasize this section on your resume. For example, if you're applying for a highly technical or specialized role requiring advanced degrees and certifications, recruiters will likely place as much weight on your education as they will your experience, if not more so (and especially if you're a recent graduate). If the role is less technical, they'll put more weight on your professional experience.

You can display your education using one of two basic formats: compact and expanded. The compact format includes every piece of information about your education in a single line. This format is a good choice for those who are further along in their careers and need to allocate more space to highlighting their professional achievements.

If you're earlier on in your career, you can use the expanded format to put more emphasis on your education. The expanded format displays the pieces of education information on separate lines, so it's a good choice for those who may have less professional experience to highlight.

There's no harm in using either one, so don't think of these as hard and fast rules—go with whatever works best for your particular situation.

Here are examples of the compact and expanded education layouts:

Compact:

EDUCATION
B.A., Marketing, Indiana University, Indianapolis, IN, 2010

Expanded:

EDUCATION
Harvard University - Cambridge, MA   **2010**
Bachelor of Arts, Biology

If you attended an elite institution such as an Ivy League, you can emphasize the school name in bold in order to draw attention to it (after all, that's why you paid the big bucks, right?). In the compact format, this means putting the school name before the degree so it doesn't look out of place on the page. An example:

EDUCATION
Harvard University - Cambridge, MA - B.A., Biology   **2010**

The city and state of the school attended should always follow the name of the school, otherwise it can lead to confusion. Keep that in mind as you experiment with the compact and expanded layouts.

The following examples demonstrate how you might depict your education for a variety of different scenarios:

GRADUATE AND UNDERGRADUATE DEGREES

Compact:

EDUCATION
Stanford Graduate School of Business, Palo Alto, CA - M.B.A.,
Entrepreneurship, 2012

Boston College, Chestnut Hill, MA - B.S., Mechanical
Engineering, 2000

In the above example, Stanford is emphasized in bold to call attention to its elite status with Boston College also appearing in bold to maintain formatting consistency. If neither were elite institutions, removing the bold emphasis would be acceptable but not necessary—both ways would work fine.

Expanded:

EDUCATION
Stanford Graduate School of Business - Palo Alto, CA   **2012**
Master of Business Administration, Entrepreneurship

Boston College - Chestnut Hill, MA   **2000**
Bachelor of Science, Mechanical Engineering

DUAL UNDERGRADUATE DEGREES FROM SAME COLLEGE

EDUCATION
Wake Forest University - Winston-Salem, NC   **1995**
B.S., Computer Science and B.S., Mathematics

DUAL UNDERGRADUATE DEGREES FROM DIFFERENT COLLEGES

EDUCATION
Wake Forest University - Winston-Salem, NC   **1998**
Bachelor of Science, Computer Science

Tulane University - New Orleans, LA   **1992**
Bachelor of Education

If you have two or more undergraduate degrees from the same school, it's best to use the expanded format because most of the time you won't have enough room to fit multiple degrees on the same line. If they're from different schools, you can include each school and degree received on separate lines with the compact format. And, you should always highlight each degree designation separately to avoid confusion. For example, if you hold a Bachelor of Science degree in both Physics and Mathematics, this should be displayed as:

B.S., Physics and B.S., Mathematics

Rather than

B.S., Physics and Mathematics

The latter example could be construed as only having one B.S. degree in "Physics and Mathematics" which undersells and miscommunicates your actual level of education.

UNDERGRADUATE DEGREE WITH MAJOR AND MINOR

Compact

EDUCATION
B.S., Mechanical Engineering with Philosophy Minor, Boston College, Chestnut Hill, MA, 2000

Expanded

EDUCATION
Boston College - Chestnut Hill, MA   **2000**
B.S., Mechanical Engineering with Philosophy Minor

UNDERGRADUATE DEGREE, PURSUING GRADUATE DEGREE

EDUCATION
University of Nebraska-Lincoln - Lincoln, NE   **Expected May 2017**
Master of Applied Science

Boston College - Chestnut Hill, MA   **2000**
Bachelor of Science, Mechanical Engineering

PURSUING UNDERGRADUATE DEGREE, NOT YET COMPLETED

EDUCATION
Virginia Tech - Blacksburg, VA   **Expected May 2018**
B.S., Physics with History Minor

HANDLING SCHOOLS AT WHICH YOU RECEIVED COLLEGE CREDIT BUT DIDN'T GRADUATE FROM

If you received college credit from one or more schools before finishing your education and graduating from a different school, you should only include the education information for the school that you graduated from. Many people take classes at a community college before completing their education at a university, which allows them to pay community college prices and still highlight the university that they graduated from on their resume. Recruiters will only care about the school name on your formal diploma, so there's no need to mention any other schools you may have attended as part of that education.

If, however, you've received college credit but didn't graduate and aren't pursuing any further education, you should include this on your resume as it will give the recruiter some sense of the level of education you've received. In these cases, it's important not to be misleading—you don't want the recruiter to get even the faintest sense that you're trying to trick them into thinking you possess a level of education that you don't.

So, rather than saying something like, "B.A., Accounting (24 Credits)", you should make it blatantly obvious that you didn't complete the degree by leading with something like "Pursued B.A. in…" or "Earned X Credits towards B.A. in…". This format makes your education status much easier to discern and removes the possibility that recruiters will think you're trying to pull a fast one.

Here's what this might look like in practice:

EDUCATION
University of Oregon - Eugene, OR   **2012 - 2014**
Earned 68 Credits towards a B.A., Accounting
Relevant Coursework - Economics, Accounting, Business, Statistics

---

Be sure to include the total number of credits received towards the degree, but only list the courses that are relevant to the role you're applying for. This will give the recruiter an accurate representation of how far your education went and how applicable your courses are to the position you're applying for. They'll be able to approximate the number of semesters you completed based on the number of credits you've earned, so no need to provide the number of semesters you attended. And, it goes without saying but it bears repeating: make sure the information you include here is 100% accurate and be prepared to present proof if necessary. Any falsifications will come out in the background check, and if you lie on any part of this, your professional credibility will take a serious hit.

HONORS, DISTINCTIONS AND SCHOLARSHIPS

If it's been less than five years since you graduated, including any honors, distinctions or scholarships you received can be an effective way of showcasing your initiative and academic capabilities. If you plan on including these, it's best to use the expanded format to highlight your education so you can list the honors or distinctions in bullets under the school information. Here's an example:

EDUCATION
University of Michigan - Ann Arbor, MI   **2008 - 2012**
Bachelor of Science, Politics
  • Graduated Summa Cum Laude with GPA 3.8/4.0
  • Dean's List 7 out of 8 semesters
  • Received Bader Scholarship for high merit

Scholarship information should also be listed in bullet form underneath the school at which it was received and as a general rule, should only be included if the job you're applying for will be your first after graduating. After your first job, employers will care less about your academic achievements and more about the results you've delivered in a professional setting, so you'll slowly want to remove academic embellishments from your resume as you advance in your career—as much as it might hurt to do so.

If you leave academic achievements on your resume for too long, you run the risk that the recruiter will think you don't have more worthy professional achievements to put in their place. It can be tough to let these go (you didn't pull all those all-nighters for nothing!) but after a certain point your professional achievements should overtake your academic ones in terms of relevance to potential employers.

If you graduated a long time ago, should you include your graduation date?

If you feel like your age is a liability for a role you're applying for, leaving off your graduation date can be an effective way to take this factor out of the equation (along with any work experience fifteen years or older). To get an idea of whether or not this may be the case, try googling the name of the company along with "average employee age". Some companies, especially those in the technology space, have a younger than average workforce where being older could be viewed as a negative. Others prefer hiring older employees for their experience and wisdom, so you may need to alter your approach depending on the situation. If you have to, make two copies of your resume with and without the graduation date and submit them where appropriate.

Technically, it's illegal for companies to discriminate by age, but there's no way you're going to prove that it happened if a potential employer simply passes on contacting you when they come across your resume. Companies are increasingly screening candidates for what they call "culture fit", which refers to how well they think a candidate would fit in with the team. Despite this practice being on the borderline of legality, many companies use it to skirt existing hiring laws. Use your best judgement when deciding whether or not to include information on your resume that would give away your age. And at the end of the day, if you're an industry veteran applying to a role on a team filled with people who are early into their careers, think about whether an environment like that is really the best fit for you.

Consistency

Make sure you're consistent in the way you display your degree information or your resume will risk looking sloppy. If you decide to abbreviate your degree designation, make sure you do so for all degrees. You don't want a recruiter to read "M.B.A." on one line and "Bachelor of Arts, Economics" on the next—they'll ding you for lack of attention to detail and you need every edge you can get.

This goes for everything else, too, like your use of the compact or expanded format, how you style things like school name and degree, and your use of bullets for embellishments. Making sure your formatting is consistent is crucial for communicating attention to detail and professionalism with your resume.

AWARDS

There are two ways to include awards you've received, and each can be more appropriate depending on the situation. The first is to list each award as a bullet under the work experience it's tied to, like so:

Google, Inc. - Mountain View, CA   **March 2013 - May 2015**
Partnerships Manager
- President's Club award for top 10% of team
  performance, Q2 2014

The second is to create a standalone section on your resume to list all your awards in one place, like this:

AWARDS
- Google - President's Club award for top 10% of team performance, Q2 2014
- Bizo - Culture Award for promoting company values, 2013 and 2014

The format you use should largely depend on the amount of content you need to fit onto your resume. If you have a ton of content to pack in, it probably wouldn't make sense to create a standalone section to list your awards as this would require a separate line for the "Awards" heading as well as spacing before and after the section. If, however, your resume is lighter on content *and* you have at least three separate awards to list, you can create a standalone section for them towards the bottom of the page preceding the education section.

Another scenario that may call for a standalone awards section is if you hold awards from non-professional organizations that you choose not to list on your resume in order to fit in professional experience. If you're a member of an organization that may not be relevant enough to highlight on your resume, but would like to mention an award that you received from it, you can include it along with other awards in a standalone section. If you don't have enough awards to warrant a standalone section, then it's best to just to leave this section off. Relevance trumps all, so if it's not something the recruiter will see as an indicator of potential success in the role, you should carefully consider whether to include it in the first place.

You need to include three key pieces of information for each award you list:

- The name of the award
- What the award was for
- When you received the award

The name of the award alone won't mean much to the recruiter reading it given that different companies will issue different awards to recognize different levels of achievement, even if they happen to have the same name. The "President's Club" at Company X is probably different from the "President's Club" at Company Y, so make sure you clearly communicate the achievement that the award recognizes. A typical format is to write the name of the award first, then the description, then the time period in which it was received. And if you list your awards in a standalone section, make sure to include the names of the companies or organizations you received them from.

Things Not to Include in Your Resume

The information you choose *not* to include in your resume is just as important as the information you *do*. Make sure *not* to include the following things on your resume, or else you'll risk taking a hit to your credibility and professionalism:

- **Objective** - For reasons already stated, including an objective statement contributes nothing to your goal of convincing your audience that you're the best fit for a particular role. You don't want the first section a recruiter sees after your contact information to be a summary of what *you* want— it's all about what *they need*, and your job is to persuade them that you're the person to give it to them. Use this primary resume real estate instead for a profile/executive summary, or jump right into your professional experience.

- **Hobbies/Interests** - It can be tempting to include areas of interest outside of work to demonstrate that you're a well-rounded individual, but most of the time doing so detracts from your resume's effectiveness. You can mention hobbies during an interview if the topic comes up, but leave them off your resume.

- **Photos** - Companies are fearful enough of employment lawsuits as it is, and you don't need to give them another reason to worry by providing anything that could be used as evidence of discrimination during the hiring process. If they really want to see what you look like, they can easily pull your LinkedIn profile, so leave this choice up to them.

- **Names of References or "References Available on Request"** - Companies typically won't ask for references until you're far along in the interview process, and by that time your resume will have already served its purpose of getting your foot in the door. When they need references, they'll ask you for them directly. No need to waste resume space on something that won't be relevant until you're already in an active conversation with a company anyway.

- **Links to social media profiles (except LinkedIn, if needed)** - It's not necessary to direct readers to your profiles on Facebook, Twitter, Instagram, Snapchat, etc.—if they're interested, recruiters will do their own stalking (this is more common than not, actually!). Including a URL for your LinkedIn profile among your contact information is acceptable, but not needed. If you do, keep it simple—drop the http://, www, and display it like this: linkedin.com/in/danclay.

- **Recommendations or Endorsements** - Some people have the idea of bringing their resume into the "modern era" by including quotes or endorsements from people they've worked with. I like this idea in theory, but a resume just isn't the place for this type of information. LinkedIn is perfect for this sort of thing, so stick to that platform for your endorsements. Once your resume piques the interest of a recruiter, they'll check out your LinkedIn profile too, so you want them to find some new information that adds to their impression of you. Don't give it all away at once!

- Personal information like age, marital status, or date of birth - **Not much to elaborate on here—leave these off.**

- Identifying characteristics such as gender, religious affiliation, or sexual orientation - **See previous bullet.**

- **Images or graphical elements** - It's true that a picture is worth a thousand words, but when it comes to a resume, the words you elicit with a picture won't be ones you want. "Unprofessional", "uninformed", "misguided", "tacky", and "waste of space" are all words a recruiter may be thinking if he sees any kind of image on your resume. Stick to words only!

- **A keywords section** - The accomplishments you bullet underneath your professional experience will already be enough to get your resume past the ATS test, so adding another standalone section just for keywords is redundant. Plus, recruiters will know what you're up to. You're better than that.

- **Desired salary or salary history** - Potential employers will ask you about this during the interview process if you get that far, so there's no need to mention it on your resume. Putting this on your resume will put you at a disadvantage in the negotiation process too, so keep this information close to the vest until it's needed.

CHAPTER 7

THE FINISHING TOUCHES

Polishing Your Resume

After you've completed the painstaking and laborious process of distilling your life's accomplishments onto a single piece of paper, it's time to put the finishing touches on your resume to make sure it stands out above the rest. It's crucial that you exercise the same attention to detail toward your resume that a Swiss watchmaker would give to the watches he produces. Every aspect of your resume needs to be infallible, down to the last period of the last sentence at the bottom of the page. Taken individually, a minor mistake may not seem like a big deal, but if there are enough of them, they can crater your chances of making it into the consideration pile—which brings me to Golden Rule number nine:

RESUME GOLDEN RULE #9
Perfection prevents rejection.

Your resume needs to be perfect, down to the last period. Keep the following rule in mind for how recruiters view mistakes: one is accidental, two are sloppy, and three are unforgivable. You're allowed *one* mistake before the recruiter starts thinking negatively about you, and even that may be a stretch. For more competitive roles, perfection is the minimum standard your resume must pass in order to keep it out of the rejection pile.

If you follow the instructions in this book, your resume will be bulletproof, ready to be held to the highest scrutiny and come out the other side just as shiny and gleaming as it went in. Pay close attention to the following areas to make sure that your resume is air tight.

Consistency

A consistent resume is a clear resume, and clarity is essential when your audience is someone who reads dozens of resumes each day. Which brings me to the final resume Golden Rule:

RESUME GOLDEN RULE #10

Be persistently consistent.

A resume that's ready for primetime demands consistency across every single element on the page. The decisions you make about how you format your resume, from the styles of your headings to your use of font emphasis, need to be consistent throughout the entire document. That means that if you use a bold, italicized, all caps 14 point font for headings, like this: ***PROFESSIONAL EXPERIENCE***, your other headings should be formatted the *exact* same way. If you italicize your job title for a position listed under your professional experience, for instance, then every other job title in your resume should be formatted in italics as well.

To go even deeper with the concept of consistency, think about the context of the information you're providing and what it means to the reader. If your job titles are italicized and the company names are in bold, then you're essentially styling "your role" in italics and "the organization" in bold. This is pretty straightforward when you're listing professional experience, but it really comes into play when you move to another section, like education. In this case, you'd want to style the name of the school in bold and your degree title in italics to match the context of your professional experience— what your role was, and where it was held. The following example underscores the point:

> **Gartner, Inc.** (organization: bold)
> *Territory Sales Manager* (role: italics)
> ...
> **Michigan State University** (organization: bold)
> *Bachelor of Arts, Marketing* (role: italics)

In the case below, formatting the education the following way would be a mistake because it breaks the consistency:

> **Bachelor of Arts, Marketing**
> *Michigan State University*

It may seem like splitting hairs, but paying attention to subtle details like this goes a long way towards putting your resume at an elite level of professionalism that's surprisingly hard to come by.

Another detail you want to make sure is consistent throughout your resume is how you write the names of the companies you've worked for. Generally, there are two ways to do this: formal and informal. The formal way spells out the full company name, i.e. "LinkedIn Corporation", while the informal way removes the entity type, i.e. "LinkedIn". One way isn't really better than the other; what's important is that you choose one and apply it consistently. Also, make sure you're consistent with your grammar—if you use the formal method and put a period at the end of "Inc.", for instance, you need to make sure there's a period after every other "Inc.", "Corp.", etc. included in your resume.

Punctuation errors are especially easy to miss on the page, so be sure to pay special attention to the tiny details. If your employment dates in the professional experience section are justified to the right side of the page, for instance, it can be difficult to discern if there are a couple spaces that may be preventing them from being perfectly aligned. The same goes with periods at the end of your bulleted achievements—those little buggers have a way of hiding out among the rest of the text in a way that's easy to overlook. The best way to check for perfect punctuation is to carefully comb through each line, starting at the top of your resume and working your way to the bottom. You should look out for extra spaces that don't belong, missing punctuation marks, weird formatting glitches (such as one bullet being mysteriously larger than the other ones on the page), and any other elements that seem out of place.

Spelling

Few things scream "unprofessional" quite as loudly as spelling errors on a resume, so pay extra close attention to avoiding these errors at all costs. A missing period is one thing, but a misspelled word will immediately take a huge bite out of your credibility that can be difficult to recover from. When a recruiter sees a spelling error, he's thinking, "if this person can't take the care to spell things right for a job they don't even have yet, what kind of care will they take when they actually have the job and we're giving them a paycheck?" I'd trade three grammar or punctuation errors for one spelling error any day, because at least the former can be excused away as an honest oversight. With spell checking functionality the norm for pretty much all word processing software, there's no excuse for even a single spelling mistake. It's a good idea to have a linguistically-inclined friend look over your resume to give you a second set of eyes to catch anything you may have missed, too—even if you have to buy him a drink in exchange for the feedback. That's a price well worth paying.

Grammar

Spelling things the right way is more straightforward than positioning the order and structure of sentences, which involves a great deal more nuance and complexity. However, if you consistently use past tense action verbs to describe your accomplishments, you shouldn't run into many sticky grammar issues.

Make sure to drop the personal pronoun from your bullets, as it's assumed that the bullets are referring to you. For example, you wouldn't say "I created a new process that reduced overhead costs by 40%", you'd simply say "Created a new process that reduced overhead costs by 40%." Including the "I" sounds weird and will actually count against you, so drop the pronouns.

Having someone else look over your resume for grammar errors will help uncover any mistakes you may have missed, and you can also use a tool like Grammarly[14] to catch things the word processor doesn't pick up. The Chrome extension is free, but if you're using a non-Google word processor like Microsoft Word you can just copy and paste the contents into a Google doc and have Grammarly point out the mistakes which you can then correct in the original document.

Tense

Pay close attention to the tense you use when outlining your achievements. If something happened in the past, make sure you describe it in the past tense. If you're currently involved with something, use the present tense to describe it. Generally speaking, the bullets you list under your previous work experience will all be in the past tense, while those you list under the position you currently hold (if you have one) may be a combination of the past and present tense. Here's an example to illustrate:

Past tense:

Designed and implemented a new document management workflow which saved the procurement department an average of three hours per week.

Present tense:

Consistently place in the top 10% of peer performance by contract value.

When using the present tense, be careful not to fall back on outlining responsibilities rather than results. If you find yourself saying something like "Manage office operations and ensure smooth meeting scheduling for chief executives", for example, that's a responsibility bullet that you'll want to reword. When in doubt, fall back to the past tense to describe concrete accomplishments. I stay away from the present tense whenever possible because of how easy it is to revert to describing responsibilities, and you may find it helpful to do the same.

Formatting

Every other formatting and stylistic element should be perfect, including spaces, tabs, line heights, font emphasis, horizontal dividers, margins, bullets, and alignments. If you need to adjust the margins to fit the amount of content on your resume, make sure you do so evenly on the left and right sides. It's okay if the top and bottom margins differ, but the side margins should be the same width, otherwise the formatting will look weird. Make sure indents are consistent throughout the resume; you can do this by clicking on the ruler mark at the top of the document (◠) to show the vertical line of the left and right margins across the screen and see where the text lines up.

Common consistency mistakes

- Single vs. double spaces at the start of a new sentence
- Abbreviating the name of a month (Dec.) in one place and writing out the full name (December) in another
- Missing periods at the end of sentences
- Improper spacing of hyphens between dates (Dec. 2011-Nov. 2012 vs. Dec. 2011 - Nov. 2012)
- Dates misaligned with the right page margin
- Incorrect use of past vs. present tense
- Inconsistent labeling of company types (LinkedIn vs. LinkedIn Corp.)
- Line spacing after some headings but not others
- Errant spaces before headings interfering with left alignment
- Random bullets sized differently than others

- Inconsistent line heights, especially before and after headings

Printing

You should always bring several printed copies of your resume to an in-person interview in case one of your interviewers asks for a copy. That means you'll need to make sure that your resume looks just as good on a printed page as it does on a computer screen.

There are two competing viewpoints when it comes to printing a resume. The first is that the paper and ink quality should be of the highest caliber, rivaling what you might see coming from the office of the President. The second viewpoint, and the one that I subscribe to, is that as long as the words appear crisply and legibly on the page, it doesn't matter much what kind of paper it's printed on as long as it's white and doesn't have any folds or creases.

In most cases, the only time you're going to use the printed version of your resume is during an in-person interview, in which case it will have already done its job of getting you in the door. Once the interview is over, the interviewer will just toss it into the trash or recycling bin anyway, so there's no sense investing in overly expensive paper. How you handle the interview will be what gets you to the next stage of the process, not the print quality of your resume.

After you print your resume, check for any smudges or spots that may have appeared during the printing process. If you find any, try printing your resume again on a fresh sheet of paper until you get a copy free of extraneous print marks. Also, make sure that none of your resume content falls outside of the print margins; if you're working with tighter margins due to a jam-packed resume, this is something you're going to have to watch out for.

Even though the content may be perfectly legible when viewed on a computer, it's important to ensure that everything translates well to a printed page in case the recruiter decides to print it—if he's unable to print your resume properly without altering the print settings, then you run the risk of making his day slightly more aggravating.

Be sure to exercise EXTREME CAUTION if you plan on printing your resume at work. In fact, I'd strongly recommend against this. Interruptions and distractions are the norm in office environments, and it's far too easy to forget about what's in the printer tray after you've pressed Control+P. Better not to take that risk in the first place than to end up in an awkward situation with your manager or peers.

File Name and Type

Use the PDF format when submitting your resume to a company or sending it as an attachment via email or any other program, unless otherwise specified by the company or recruiter. All word processing programs will have the option to save a document as a PDF, so this shouldn't be difficult. The only time you should use the raw document format is if you're editing the document yourself or sending it to someone else to make edits for you.

When uploading your resume through a company's careers page, make sure the information transfers over correctly as the software has a tendency to butcher resume content (go figure, right?). If the software continues to turn your resume into gibberish from a PDF or Word document, try uploading it as a plain text file if the system allows and see if that helps.

Before submitting your resume, you'll want to rename the file to something descriptive that helps both you and any recruiters keep track of it more easily. As your resume evolves with the advancement of your career, it helps to have each version of your resume saved with a different filename in order to keep track of what you're adding and taking away with each iteration. Plus, it's always fun to look back on what your resume used to look like in the early stages of your career and marvel at how far you've come!

When assigning a file name to your resume, make sure to include your first and last name along with the month and year of the most recent saved version. If you finish the latest version of your resume in August 2016, for example, the name of the file might be "Dan Clay Resume_August 2016". Including the date in the file name will help you keep track of the different versions you have saved as well as communicate to the recruiter that the resume is a recent version.

When you submit your resume to a company, make sure the date in the file name matches up with the date on which you submit it. This not only indicates that your resume is fresh, but it also sends a signal to the recruiter that you're early in the job search process and are a hot commodity that will be snatched up soon (even if you've actually been on the job hunt for awhile).

If the date in the file name is for six months prior, for instance, the recruiter might wonder why you've been unsuccessful getting any offers since beginning your job search and may automatically think that there's something the other companies know about you that they shouldn't waste time to figure out for themselves. Job searches often take several months before they result in an offer, and that's okay—but you don't need to broadcast this information to recruiters.

A final touch you may consider is to include the name of the company you're applying to in the name of the file, like "Dan Clay Resume_August 2016_Gartner". This helps you keep track of the different versions you may be submitting for each company and communicates to the recruiter that the version they're seeing was made just for them. Even if you're submitting the same resume to each company you apply to, changing the file name to reflect each individual company can be a nice touch that requires relatively little effort to customize.

CHAPTER 8

BRINGING IT ALL TOGETHER

Writing a resume can seem like a trite formality that shouldn't be necessary in today's age of digital and social media, but it's one of the most worthwhile investments you can make into your career. Having a resume that stands above the rest is something to be proud of and can provide a huge confidence boost throughout the job search process. And confidence is key—without it, you'll be stuck waiting for things to happen to you rather than taking the steps to make them happen yourself.

The resources included with this book are designed to make the resume creation process as straightforward and painless as possible. If you're having trouble coming up with great action verbs to showcase your professional achievements, refer to the *77 Hard-Hitting Resume Action Verbs and Phrase Examples* to get the creative juices flowing. Each action verb includes an example of how it can be used in context, and they can also be copied and pasted into your formal resume structure and modified to fit your specific achievements. Don't worry about plagiarism, either—these are here for you to borrow and steal from as needed (as long as they're truthful, of course)!

I also encourage you to use one of the five pre-built resume templates included as resources in this guide. I've personally used a variation of these to land the lucrative positions I've held and helped friends and acquaintances land their dream jobs with them as well. There's no sense re-creating something that's already been proven to work, so spend your time developing your content and use one of the templates for the formatting. Word of caution, though: steer clear of Microsoft

Word resume templates; recruiters will be able to spot them from a mile away.

 And before you consider your resume complete, be sure to double check your work with the **66 Point Perfect Resume Checklist** available for free at www.danclay.com/perfectresume!

In Closing

Remember, you're much better than you give yourself credit for. How you view yourself and your capabilities will have a tremendous impact on how successful you are in the job search and interview process, so developing a positive attitude is key. Your attitude will shine through in everything from the tone of your resume to the emails you send recruiters—make sure it exudes the traits of someone they'd be crazy not to want to interview and learn more about.

I hope you've found this book helpful, and I wish you the best of luck as you embark on your job search journey—although the better your resume is, the less luck you'll need!

For ongoing advice and guidance on how to mindfully navigate your career for maximum happiness and fulfillment, subscribe to The Conscious Career newsletter on danclay.com and follow me on LinkedIn at www.linkedin.com/in/danclay.

Go get 'em!

Cheers, Dan

DON'T FORGET TO DOWNLOAD YOUR FREE BONUS MATERIALS!

Now that you know how to construct your own perfect resume, it's time to put your newfound knowledge into practice. Visit the companion website at www.danclay.com/perfectresume to download everything you need to start building your resume, including:

- Five customizable, fully editable resume templates in Microsoft Word format that have been tested and proven to land interviews at world-class organizations

- 77 Hard-Hitting Resume Action Verbs and Phrase Examples in PDF format to help you build powerful resume bullets that will instantly grab attention

- The 66-Point Perfect Resume Checklist in PDF format to make sure your resume is absolutely perfect before sending to recruiters and hiring managers

- A Before & After Resume Transformation example to see the difference between a resume that recruiters pass over versus one they can't ignore

To access these **FREE** bonus materials, simply visit www.danclay.com/perfectresume, enter your name and email address, and click the button to submit.

ONE LAST THING...

I know you have many choices when it comes to the books you read, and I'm extremely grateful that you chose to read this one.

Seriously—thank you!

I just have one small favor to ask: **Please take a minute or two to review this book on Amazon.**

Your feedback will help ensure that I continue to write the kinds of books that deliver results for readers like you, which is something I strive to do every time I sit down and put words on the page.

And if you want to get in touch, feel free to drop me a line at dan@danclay.com—I'd love to hear from you!

REFERENCES

[1]   Top HR Statistics, https://www.glassdoor.com/employers/popular-topics/hr-stats.htm

[2]   http://www.forbes.com/sites/jacquelynsmith/2013/08/09/the-25-companies-that-give-the-most-difficult- job-interviews/#4923d0ed5b76

[3]   http://www.inc.com/peter-economy/19-interesting-hiring-statistics-you-should-know.html

[4]   http://www.eremedia.com/ere/why-you-cant-get-a-job-recruiting-explained-by-the-numbers/

[5]   http://www.careerbuilder.com/share/aboutus/pressreleasesdetail.aspx?sd=7/11/2012&id=pr707&ed=12/31/2012

[6]   http://www.businessinsider.com/nina-mufleh-airbnb-resume-2015-4

[7]   https://www.huffingtonpost.com/entry/airbnb-resume-viral_us_55a90cb3e4b0c5f0322d0b5a

[8] http://www.businessinsider.com/the-resume-that-got-nina-mufleh-job-interviews-with-uber-linkedin-and-airbnb-2015-7

[9] http://www.magiceye.com/

[10] http://fundamentum.com/how-long-employers-spend-looking-at-your-resume-and-what-to-do-about-it/

[11] https://dl.acm.org/citation.cfm?id=2996745&dl=ACM&coll=DL

[12] http://business.time.com/2012/04/13/how-to-make-your-resume-last-longer-than-6-seconds/

[13] http://money.cnn.com/2012/05/13/technology/yahoo-ceo-out/

[14] https://www.grammarly.com/

Made in the USA
Middletown, DE
02 February 2021